Beverly Sheppard
Editor

**Pennsylvania Federation
of Museums and
Historical Organizations**

AMERICAN ASSOCIATION OF MUSEUMS

Acknowledgements

Building Museum and School Partnerships evolved from education workshops sponsored by the Pennsylvania Federation of Museums and Historical Organizations in 1991. The Federation wishes to thank the contributing authors and the editor for the knowledge, skill and expertise which they brought to the project.

The publication of *Building Museum and School Partnerships* was made possible, in part, by grants from the Institute of Museum Services and the Pennsylvania Department of Education and by support from the Pennsylvania Historical and Museum Commission.

Reprinted and distributed by American Association of Museums, 1997
1575 Eye St. N.W., Suite 400, Washington, D.C. 20005: (202) 289-1818:
Fax (202) 289-6578.

ISBN: 0-931201-18-7

Pennsylvania Federation of Museums and Historical Organizations,
P.O. Box 1026, Harrisburg, PA 17108-1026

Phone: (717) 787-3253 or 787-1902; Fax: (717) 783-1073

Foreword

One of my earliest and most memorable learning experiences was with a few pieces of shard that my father put into my five-year-old hand as he told me about the Indians who worked the clay into pots. Close inspection showed finger prints of the "real" person who had handled the soft clay a long, long time ago. To say I was impressed is an understatement, because that experience with a piece of pottery, a primary source — "the real thing" — lives with me today. Learning made vital and interesting by association with objects, powerful metaphor, or deep cultural meaning most certainly should be playing to the many thousands of students that attend Pennsylvania's schools.

Every crossroads, village, town and city in Pennsylvania can boast of a history that helps to define the ideas and issues of our culture today. The museums and historical associations that abound in Pennsylvania are the caretakers of this heritage. There are hundreds and hundreds of such museums, large and small. Yet, the artifacts and documents they contain and the people and places they enshrine are often unknown and unseen by people who live just short distances away. Their educational potential goes unused.

A modest effort to share the learning resources of small and rural museums with their educational communities began in my office when note was made of the extraordinary quality of art exhibitions offered at the Southern Alleghenies Museum of Art, an autonomous museum located on the grounds of St. Francis College in rural Loretto, Pennsylvania.

With modest funding from the Pennsylvania Department of Education and cooperation from the Association of Rural and Small Schools, as well as strong support from the Art Education Department at Penn State and the Southern Alleghenies Museum of Art, a series of meetings were held to explore the possibilities for museum and school collaborations. Teachers, students, school directors, principals, professors and museum leaders joined the exciting dialogue and addressed ways to delineate our broad concerns and focus on how to make programmatic development and partnerships a reality. From these concerns came a dynamic Institute for teachers and museum leaders led by Dr. Robert Ott in the summer of 1991 at St. Francis College. The evaluations and recommendations that grew from that Institute will be used as future work unfolds.

The Pennsylvania Federation of Museums and Historical Organizations assumed the mantle of leadership following the Institute, organizing and presenting three workshops for museum educators and teachers across the state to continue the development of museum and school collaborations. The issues addressed in these workshops form the core content of this publication, which organizes many voices to address both the ideals and the practices of working together.

The potential for solid, meaningful and productive partnerships between educational agencies and museums — *large and small* — that preserve and interpret art, science and history must be nurtured for the future. Such partnerships can indeed be made — perhaps not as easily as a father who simply presses an Indian shard into a young boy's hand and says, "Do you see that...." However, the work is certainly not beyond our abilities.

Clyde M. McGeary, Retired
Division of Arts and Sciences
Pennsylvania Department of Education

Table of Contents

The Perfect Mix: Museums and Schools

Beverly Sheppard

Associate Director, Chester County Historical Society

Education has become the "hot topic" of the museum world. Museum education has had a long history in American museums, but it has frequently been at the periphery of the museum's stated mission. The "landmark document" *Excellence and Equity*, the first major report on the educational role of museums ever to be issued by the American Association of Museums (AAM), has shifted education to the center of the museum's concerns.

One of the report's key concepts states, "...the educational role of museums is at the core of their service to the public. This assertion must be clearly stated in every museum's mission and central to every museum's activities." *Excellence and Equity* defines the museum's educational mission as a "museum-wide endeavor" that makes a commitment to excellence in all facets of the institution's public service.

The 1984 Report of the Commission on Museums for a New Century, also published by AAM, likewise underscores the significance of the museum's educational role, asserting that, "If collections are the heart of museums, what we have come to call education — the commitment to presenting objects

Students encounter the magic of the "real" when they visit museums.

and ideas in an informative and stimulating way — is the spirit." Museum professionals are challenged by this report, as well as by *Excellence and Equity*, to use our educational facilities to "...communicate ideas, impart knowledge, encourage curiosity and promote aesthetic sensibility."

Museum educators have long understood the inherent educational power of collections and the ideas they represent. Our experiences have demonstrated the impact of encounters with the real. As we accept the challenge to provide educational leadership within our institutions, it is appropriate to begin with one of the oldest and most successful aspects of museum education — the museum and school partnership.

Museum and school partnerships have a long history. *Museums for a New Century* refers to this history as, "...perhaps the most longstanding and successful example of the interest and ability of museums to join forces with other institutions in working toward common goals."

Museums and schools are natural partners. They offer complementary experiences, combining two languages of learning —the words of the classroom and the objects of the museum. Their educators offer two kinds of expertise — classroom teaching methods and visual learning techniques. Together they can present students with an enriching partnership of ideas, discovery, challenge and fun, a partnership well worth developing and sustaining.

There is nothing like the real thing. No textbook account, video image, computer simulation or recorded sound can ever match the wonder of the real. When students enter a historic site, gaze at a distant star, or stand before a work of art, they encounter the object, place or experience described on the pages of their texts. This is the "magic" of museums, the special ingredient museums bring to the educational experience.

The Field Museum publication, *Teach the Mind, Touch the Spirit*, describes the drama of a museum visit in the following words: "Like a balloon that once blown up never shrinks to its former size, the dimensions of a child's world are forever enlarged by a visit to a museum." A balloon is at its best soaring free, but first it must be transformed from a tight, constricted shape. It must be loosened and stretched, made pliable and responsive, and once, so affected, can continue to grow and expand. A well-designed museum visit has the potential of becoming such a pivotal experience in a child's lifelong learning.

Museums are compelling environments. They offer a tangible dimension to learning, engaging the senses and stimulating inquiry. The common denominator in all museum education is that in museums we communicate ideas through objects. Objects have a great deal of power. They can allure and entrance; they can provoke new questions and insights. Our job as museum educators is to facilitate the interaction between students and objects. We need to teach the visual and perceptual skills that engage students in sensory learning — encouraging them to look, examine, compare, contrast, collect data, analyze and evaluate. This visual approach to learning offers a distinct complementary experience to the classroom where the learning vocabulary is primarily verbal.

Young children learn by sensory examination. Toddlers see, hear, touch, taste and smell their worlds. Within a short time, the development of language abilities replaces much of this kind of exploration. A child's life is increasingly dominated by verbal and logistical thinking skills. Reality is additionally filtered by the proliferation of media which have become the intermediaries for direct sensory experience. *Our children live in a world with lots of information but little encounter.* Few have much experience with how things work, how they were made or how extraordinary it is to create something of value with their own hands. *Museums remain one of the few environments where encounter is the basis for learning.*

A personal story taught me the impact of a firsthand encounter. Several years ago the orbit of Halley's comet brought it close to the earth. It was barely visible in the night sky, but I was intrigued by the rarity of seeing this event. I set out on a cold winter evening with a star map, a pair of binoculars and the memory of a wonderful book, *The Invisible Pyramid* by Loren Eiseley. Eiseley had written about how his father had held the young boy in his arms and pointed out the comet soaring overhead. He told the child that the comet would not reappear until young Eiseley was an old man himself but asked that he look for it again for both of them.

From that moment on, the author was always aware of the orbit of the comet, charting time by its rhythm. Eiseley died shortly before its return, but his story stayed with me. It was now my time in history to see the comet.

It was so cold that my hands shook, making it nearly impossible for me to see through the binoculars. I finally succeeded by propping them against my car on the dark road I had chosen for my observatory. At first I saw only a tiny light like a fuzzy tennis ball among the other brighter constellations. I confirmed it to be the comet by going out successive evenings and charting its movement. I was exhilarated. The light was never dazzling, but I was witnessing firsthand a bit of the universe I had known only through books, a phenomenon I would never see again.

Not long afterward I told my adventure to a friend, right down to the frigid weather and shaking hands. My friend listened to me puzzled and impatient. "You really must be crazy," he eventually concluded. "Why would you go through all of that when there were dozens of specials on television? You would have seen the comet up close, learned more about it, and stayed warm!"

My friend may well have been able to quote more facts about Halley's comet, but I had seen it firsthand, and my encounter made me more powerfully aware of the universe than any book I had ever read or any television program I had ever seen.

This is the power of encounter that museums can offer. We can introduce students to new understandings through the magic of the real — the real paintings, the actual documents, the tangible artifacts of another era, the specimens of science — leading them from object to understanding.

To do this successfully, we need schools as our partners. There is a kind of synergistic relationship between classroom learning and museum experiences. No one is more expert about the students themselves than their teacher. The teacher's sensitivity to the needs of students, their learning styles, abilities, and interests is an asset we cannot do without. The museum teacher's familiarity with the collections, the ideas inherent in them and the nature of object-based teaching is the other half of the equation for successful programming.

A successful partnership begins with communication. We must identify how to share our common goals with schools and how to establish the beginnings of an effective dialogue. Our partnership must include administrative support as well as teacher interest, for our ultimate aim is to establish museums as integral components in the total educational experience. Intelligent and well-administered programming is the key to gaining administrative commitment.

This publication will examine the ingredients of the effective museum-school partnership: how we achieve it, maintain it and evaluate its success. The book will address both logistics and theory. It will examine the schools' expectations of the museum and what the museum can request in turn and will look at ways to bring teachers into both planning and presenting. It will define the nature of focused field trips and the components of pre-visit preparation, hands-on exploration and post-visit activities. The writers will also look at alternatives to field trips — the nature of outreach programs, from traveling trunks to itinerant speakers — and programs that use the community as classroom. Finally the book will explore the theoretical bases of teaching in the museum setting, including an examination of current learning theories, a case study of teaching critical thinking skills, and the use of the museum as an environment for teaching cultural diversity. The book includes extensive bibliographies and an appendix of forms, formats and program ideas.

Beyond the reading is the application of these ideas. There is no substitute for inspired teaching and effective collaboration. The museum and school partnership is the product of educators working together to realize the common goals of presenting students with vibrant, meaningful and engaging learning. Let a museum and school partnership introduce your museum as a provocative educational resource to return to again and again.

References

Excellence and Equity: Education and the Public Dimension of Museums. American Association of Museums, adopted as a policy statement by AAM, 1991.

Museums for a New Century, A Report of the Commission on Museums for a New Century, American Association of Museums. Washington, DC: American Association of Museums, 1984.

Voris, Helen H., Maija Sedzielarz, Carolyn Blackmon. *Teach the Mind, Touch the Spirit*. Chicago, IL: Field Museum of Natural History, 1986.

What Do Schools Want From Museums?

Fred D. Richter, Ph.D.

Director of Elementary Education,
Lebanon (Pennsylvania) School District

Collaborative partnerships must begin with a clear understanding of the common goals of the collaboration as well as the specific needs of each partner. A survey of over 200 teachers in Chester County asked teachers what they expected from museum visits. Over 65% responded that an understanding of the students and a tolerant manner were most important.

In the following chapter, a school administrator provides insight into today's students and the expectations their teachers have for museum visits. His review of effective teaching techniques makes clear the need for school teachers and museum teachers to work together.

Introduction

The writer took surveys in 1989 and 1991 to determine what public school educators and children expected when they visited a museum with their classes. The expectations can be placed into two broad categories: **educational** (e.g. types of exhibitions and programs) and **logistical** (e.g. clean, accessible lavatories, short waits, child-sized water fountains, etc.).

The changing face of society adds another dimension to working with 1990s school children. This chapter will outline some of the differences between today's children and those in the past and will identify teachers' educational and logistical expectations. Perhaps in the end, more questions will have been raised than answered. However, these questions must be considered if museums are to be successful learning environments in the twenty-first century.

The educational desires of teachers visiting museums may be placed in two categories — learning and enjoyment. Teachers expect their classes to learn something about a topic they are studying in school, but they also want

children to find museums fun. Teachers, as well as museum professionals, want children to think enough of their visit that they will return to the museum on their own. Adapting to the educational needs of the 1990s is imperative if these expectations are to be met.

Our Changing Society

Today's children are different from those of the past. Herbert Zimiles found them more *worldly, self-assured, verbal, assertive and impulsive, but less disciplined, organized and conforming.* "In the past they (children) would seldom interrupt an adult, but now they do so as a matter of course." (Zimiles, 1986, p.6)

In the 1980s President Reagan talked about a social safety net to protect every American from societal ills. Today, it seems America has passed on what Charlotte, the friendly spider, recounted in *Charlotte's Web* (E.B. White, 1952). "A web gets torn every day by the insects that kick around in it, and a spider must rebuild it when it gets full of holes...." Our social net is full of holes, and it is not being rebuilt.

Statistics about today's children can be grim. Traditional families with two married parents accounted for only 56% of all households in 1989, a drop of 71% since 1970. The average time parents spend with their families dropped from thirty hours a week in 1965 to seventeen hours a week today. The Family Research Council estimates that only four and a half minutes of that seventeen hours is spent in meaningful conversation.

While parent contacts drop, television time increases until the television now exceeds parents (twenty hours weekly to seventeen hours) as their children's most frequent companion. Who is teaching our children values? Is it the television that broadcasts 18.4 acts of violence per hour so that the average child has witnessed 200,000 maimed and murdered people by the time he reaches his sixteenth birthday?

Are we surprised that the FBI found arrest for children under eighteen for murder and aggravated assault increased over 20% in the last five years or that one of every five school children carries a gun to school or that teachers in Oakland, California (November 18, 1991) walked off the job, not for more pay, but for more security guards?

Or, perhaps more disturbing are the teen suicide numbers from the Centers for Disease Control: one in twelve high school students tried to commit suicide in the past year, and more than one in four seriously contemplated it. The suicide rate has quadrupled in four decades.

A study by the Fullerton, California Police Department (1988) found marked changes in leading school discipline problems today and forty years ago. The problems most often encountered by teachers were:

1940s	1980s
- Talking	- Drug abuse
- Chewing gum	- Alcohol abuse
- Making noise	- Pregnancy
- Running in the halls	- Suicide
- Getting out of line	- Rape
- Wearing improper clothes	- Robbery
- Not putting paper in basket	- Assault

The purpose of citing this data is not to depress the reader, but to give sharp focus to the differences between today's children and those of the not-so-distant past. An environment defined by computers, Nintendo, the media, dysfunctional families and unprecedented drug-infested households is different from the past. To meet the needs of the twenty-first-century child, schools and museums must also be different from the past.

The results of both the 1989 and 1991 surveys cited at the beginning of this chapter were clear. Teachers want children to learn and to enjoy their museum experiences. It is essential that the demographics are not forgotten as the difficult tasks of meeting teacher expectations is begun.

Educational Experiences

Research on retention has repeatedly shown that we tend to learn more in environments that are free from tension. Nummela and Rosengren (1986) in their studies have found, "The most comprehensive learning includes an

absence of threat, careful orchestration of multidimensional teaching strategies, real-life experiences and an understanding of barriers to learning." The time in the museum must be enjoyable. Enjoyment not only increases retention, but also makes it more likely that the visitor will return.

— PENNSYLVANIA ACADEMY OF THE FINE ARTS

Having fun is an important part of the learning experience. Inspired by some 19th-century narrative paintings, students enjoy telling their own stories at the Pennsylvania Academy of the Fine Arts.

Marilyn Hood (1991) in her research summary, *Misconceptions Held by Museum Professionals*, noted that "Hundreds of people have come (to museums) once and have no intention of returning if they had a disappointing experience." Hood also stated, "...as many school children are turned off to museums for life as are intrigued by them because of unsatisfactory experiences they have had on school tours."

Children develop what Lillian Katz (1988) has called dispositions. Dr. Katz has defined a disposition as a habit of the mind, a tendency to act in a certain way in a certain situation. Dispositions are learned, as are basic facts. Growing up we learn such dispositions as curiosity, humor or generosity. We might also learn such dispositions as unfriendliness, avarice or callousness.

What museum professionals must not forget is that as children parade through their facilities learning facts, ideas and concepts, they are also learning dispositions. The learning cannot be separated from the disposition, for whether we choose to deal with dispositions or not, they are there. Nummela and Rosengren (1986) note, "Learning occurs *constantly* (emphasis added) at both the conscious and unconscious levels." In truth, the dispositions last far longer than the factual information. *A positive experience must **never** be sacrificed for the sake of adding more facts.*

Poorly run museum tours are hit with the "double whammy effect" — not only don't children learn, but they also don't want to return in the future to learn. Indeed, it would be far better in the long term to cancel museum visits when conditions are less than ideal than to bring a group in and allow them to have an unsatisfactory experience.

One caveat: enjoyment is the by-product of good instruction; it is not a goal. The goal of a trip to a movie theater is enjoyment. The goal of a museum visit is learning. Enjoyment, however, follows good instruction and will create the desired disposition to return to the museum for both pleasure and learning.

The overlap between retention and enjoyment spreads throughout the learning paradigm. One of the variables of retention in Madeline Hunter's (1985) effective teaching work is a **positive climate**. Hunter's other variables include: **transfer**, **practice**, and **meaning**.

Without doing justice to the comprehensiveness of Dr. Hunter's work, I include the following. If children are to leave the museum with a maximum amount of learning, these learning variables must be considered:

Transfer

Something learned in one context is used in a different context. There are two basic types of transfer: one is a very basic transfer such as how learning to drive a Ford would help when driving a Honda; the other is a more complex type which does **not** happen automatically. If a child learns a skill in school, it might not be transferred to the museum environment. Conscious efforts must be made by school and museum professionals to bridge the learning gap. *Items to be transferred must be referred to and the relationship between them must be specifically demonstrated.*

Practice

Most people must review a fact or concept a number of times before it is retained. What researchers have found is that the so-called "spacing effect" increases retention. The information a student got from cramming for a test is soon forgotten, while information learned at regular intervals can be retained far longer — if not for life.

Spreading discussions of the museum topic over several days or weeks reinforces the importance of museum-school cooperation. That each knows what the other is doing and that children have an opportunity to discuss their museum visit both before and afterward greatly increases the likelihood that the museum learning will be retained.

Meaning

The most powerful retention variable and perhaps the one most often over-looked is meaning. The more meaning something has, the more easily it is retained. The more something relates to one's personal experience, the more it is retained. Children must be able to relate their learning experiences to themselves — a task made easier through direct interaction.

Interactions for children can come on three basic levels: with an adult, with each other, or with the environment. The children should be involved, active and expressive, not passive and receptive (Katz and Chard, 1989).

Underlying the importance of meaningfulness is the fact that what is mean-ingful to one person is not necessarily meaningful to another. World War II might be an exciting time for a docent, but may have absolutely no meaning to a class of five-year-olds. It becomes essential either to create meaning or to be flexible enough to move on to something else. The visit should stress quality over quantity.

In summary, the goals of the museum visit are to optimize the simultane-ous acquisition of knowledge and desirable dispositions. Skills without the disposition to use them are unproductive; dispositions without skills are frus-trating (Katz and Chard, 1989).

Logistical Expectations

In the 1989 and 1991 surveys, the second broad area of teacher desires was subsumed under the rubric *logistical needs* and included most things that might be considered physical comforts. The overlaps between this area and the educational area are obvious when we review the importance of dispositions.

A child's desire to return to the museum could be sullied because he couldn't find the restroom or he spilled a beverage while sitting at a table too

high for him in the lunchroom. The program itself could have been a finely tuned educational experience, but failure to attend to a child's logistical needs could spoil the best of educational experiences.

Teachers identified five logistical needs on their surveys.

- Children-sized lunchrooms, water fountains and lavatory facilities
- Low-priced educational items in the gift shop, items that represent museum themes — not trinkets
- Elimination of management problems like standing in lines or having children wait with nothing to do
- Guides who are knowledgeable about the museum materials as well as working with the learning skills of each specific age level
- A high-quality, focused experience, not just viewing a lot of things (in other words, looking for quality not quantity)

Children's Expectations

Children were also surveyed. As with the teachers, the children's concerns were easily clustered into several key areas. The children wanted:

- **To touch things.** Involving more senses than just the visual increases learning and interest (Manly, 1989). One student wrote, "I don't like it when you cannot touch the stuff. They act like one touch and it is gonna fall apart." Reasons should be given as to why some things cannot be touched, but interactive opportunities should be part of the visit.
- **To not have their guides talk too much.** A fifth grader put it very succinctly, "I don't like it when the guides talk forever." Remember, telling is not teaching.
- **To not have the guides rush them.** Sometimes children like to look longer at things they find interesting. Ironically, the better job the guide does at connecting with children's interests, the more of a problem this becomes.
- **To not have to be quiet too much.** Children, especially young children, learn through interacting with adults and each other. A sixth grade girl wrote, "The museums I don't like are the ones where you have to be just as quiet as a mouse." Too much talking by guides, rushing and not letting children talk are all characteristics of seeking quantity rather than quality. There certainly are times for guides to talk and for children to be quiet, but the question is for how much time?
- **To be able to see from a crowd.** Ushered through the museum in groups, many children do not see what is being discussed. A fourth grade boy noted, "I don't like it when there is no room and you get crowded and people start to push you out of the way." Another boy wrote, "And last but not least. I really hated when you are bunched up and you can't see a thing." Consider the group size and children's sizes when visual contact is important.

The majority of children were very supportive of museums in their responses. Two comments sum up their feelings quite well. One boy wrote, "What I liked least was really nothing," and a fourth grader got quickly to the point, "The museum was great."

Conclusion

Museums offer schools excellent models. In "Making Schools More Like Museums," Howard Gardner (1991) writes, "If we are to configure an education for understanding, suitable for the students of today and for the world of tomorrow, we need to take the lessons of the museum...to think of the ways in which the museum atmosphere...can pervade all educational environments."

Museum-school partnerships can benefit both parties, but best of all can benefit children, "...if educators and museum personnel work together to make the visits exciting learning experiences. The plan is simple — planning, follow-up, and cooperation." (Linder, 1987)

References

Fullerton, CA Police Department. In Bowen, E. "Getting Tough," *Time*, February 1, 1988, 52-58.

Gardner, H. "Making Schools More Like Museums," *Education Week*, 6, 6: October 9, 1991.

Hood, M. "Misconceptions Held by Museum Professionals," *Visitor Behavior*, 6, 1991, 1:4-6.

Hunter, M. *Retention Theory for Teachers*. El Segundo, California: TIP Publications, 1985.

Katz, L. and S.C. Chard. *Engaging Children's Minds: The Project Approach*. Norwood, NJ: Ablex Publishing Co., 1989.

Katz, L. "Early Education: What Should Young Children Be Doing?" *Texas Elementary Principals and Supervisors Association Journal*, 37, Spring, 1988: 12-15.

Linder, B. "Museum-School Partnerships." NASSP Bulletin, December 1987, 122-24.

Manly, H. "How Kids Learn." *Newsweek*, April 17, 1989, Special Report.

Nummela, R. and T. Rosengren. "What's Happening in Students' Brains May Redefine Teaching." *Educational Leadership*, 43, 1986, 8: 49-53.

White, E.B. *Charlotte's Web*. New York: Scholastic, 1952.

Zimiles, H. "The Social Context of Early Childhood in an Era of Expanding Preschool Education." In *Today's Kindergarten*, edited by Bernard Spodek. New York: Teacher College Press, 1986.

What Do Museums Want From Schools?

Beverly Sheppard

Classroom teachers and museum educators share the common goal of presenting vibrant, meaningful and pleasurable learning experiences to children. When museums and schools come together to plan new programs, they bring different skills, styles and needs into the partnership. Just as schools need to communicate their expectations to museums, museums must be very clear about what they want from schools. The following chapter addresses the methods and tools museum educators can use to make their expectations clear. Good partnering begins with good communication.

The Scenario

Two busloads, totalling nearly 100 students, unload at their field trip destination. The students, hoarse from shouting and gleeful from horseplay, emerge in unruly groups. They are not really sure where they are. They certainly don't know why they are there. They are hot, wrinkled, and their lunches are soggy, and worst of all, they are eighth graders! The museum staff cowers in the door. One breaks out in hives. They all take a deep breath before greeting the mobs. This is the field trip as *ordeal*.

How often have museum educators complained that teachers take field trips as a "day off," leaving them with unprepared and poorly disciplined students? Anyone who has undergone the teacher's trauma of arranging a field trip, badgering students for permission slips, collecting money and fighting administrative restrictions knows that the field trip begins as a hassle for teachers. Yet, why does this same teacher who undergoes the heroic effort of setting up a field trip, often seem to "let go" at the door of the museum?

Many teachers who are very comfortable in their classrooms are equally insecure in a museum gallery. They are the experts on their students' learning skills and curriculum needs, but they expect you to be the experts on the museum collections and the ideas inherent in them. They view their part in the museum and school collaboration as getting their students through your doors, and they expect you to know what to do once the students have arrived. The aim of the museum-school partnership, however, is to bring the classroom teacher and the museum educator together — not just physically, but intellectually as well.

In *Collaborative Programs: Museums and Schools* (1980) Alberta Sebolt notes, "Collaboration means you are willing to work together to create, develop, design and implement a program which you both want. Most of all, collaboration means a promise of time spent in learning about and from each other, while planning a program to address learner needs through clearly defined objectives."

Some of our relationships with schools will achieve the objective of total collaborative planning. Others will be one-time visits, perhaps repeated annually. Yet, each field trip experience can be made far more effective if museums communicate their needs and expectations clearly.

The Program Brochure

The first communication with the teacher is often the program brochure designed and mailed by the museum. The brochure may be a high-styled, multi-page booklet or it may be a xeroxed page. Like all written material targeted for a specific audience, the design should reflect the intent of the publication. Who will receive and use the brochure? What information will they require? How will it be distributed?

The primary purpose of the program brochure is to inform teachers about the programs offered and the logistics of making reservations. The brochure also allows the museum to express its personality and set the tone for the anticipated visit. Remember that teachers receive a great deal of mail; design your brochure to be attractive and distinctive *(see Brochure Content Checklist on page 17).*

Distribution of school brochures poses additional problems. Mailing costs are very high, so it is wise to target appropriate teachers as

Museums want schools to understand how children learn in gallery settings and how well-planned field trips can complement the classroom experience.

Brochure Content Checklist

In addition to strong design, a good brochure has several key components. Use the following checklist.

- **Introduction of the museum.** Establish your identity clearly. Who are you? What are your collections? What topics are represented in your collections that relate to school needs? Why should teachers bring their students to you?

- **Description of your educational programs.** Do you offer outreach programs? traveling trunks? focused lessons? teacher in-service? List the topics of your programs and give an enticing description.

- **Grade level recommendations.** Age and grade levels targeted by each program should be clearly indicated in the text. Let teachers know that you address programs to specific age and skill levels.

- **Time programs are offered.** Include seasonal information as well as hours and days of the week.

- **Recommended length of programs.** Let teachers anticipate their needs for buses and other scheduling concerns.

- **Recommended group size.** Are there any limitations on group size?

- **Additional facilities.** Do you have eating facilities? a museum shop appropriate for children? parking facilities?

- **Program fees.** Do you offer a single program fee or are fees charged per child? Is there an admission charge for teachers and chaperones also?

- **Accessibility.** Are you accessible to visitors with disabilities? Is the accessible entrance clearly marked?

- **Chaperones.** Do you require a specific number of chaperones or a ratio of adults to students?

- **Reservation information.** How do you make a reservation? What information will teachers need to have in hand when calling? Do not make teachers search for your phone number. It is wise to repeat it in several areas.

- **Directions.** A map and/or written directions is especially valuable and might also be sent with pre-visit materials.

- **Special requirements.** Some museums establish basic behavioral guidelines in their program brochures. Such information as "Photography not allowed" may be especially useful. However, a forbidding tone may discourage visitors.

specifically as possible. After all your effort in developing a program brochure, you certainly do not want it to disappear into the "black hole" of the school's central office. Some teachers suggest sending a packet to the school secretary. Follow up with a phone call soliciting his/her help in distribution. If individual teachers' names are not known, it is helpful to address brochures to "Third Grade Teacher," "Seventh Grade Social Studies Teacher," etc. If you cannot afford to print or mail a large number of brochures, research the names of department heads and send a packet accompanied by a personal letter.

In most counties of Pennsylvania, the district Intermediate Unit has an established delivery system. Discuss with officials in the Intermediate Unit the possibility of delivering your brochures through their system. It will require labeling and packaging according to delivery codes, but the savings in postage is well worth the additional effort.

Brochures designed as self-mailers also save extra labor. Keep a supply on hand to meet special requests. A brochure should be designed with a lifetime of at least two years. Inexpensive program updates can always be tucked inside.

Reservation Information

A single phone call may be your only contact with a school group before it arrives. Both your expectations and those of the teacher and students may well be established in these few moments. Even though your program brochure is very explicit, be thorough in the questions you ask and the information you write down (*see **Designing a Reservation Form** on page 19*).

Before you complete your conversation, you may wish to advise the teacher about any special rules or regulations. Teachers may have misconceptions about proper museum behavior. One group visiting Chester County Historical Society had been told by their teacher that they could not talk while in the museum. They were to treat it like a library. The museum educator struggled to get the students involved in an opening activity before she realized the problem. The telephone conversation and the pre-visit materials can both set the behavioral expectations — from who is responsible for disciplining to what hands-on rules may apply.

Place the date of the planned visit in the upper-right-hand corner of the reservation form, along with the initials of the person taking the reservation. This will make it easy to file and check on when necessary. The reservation form can also include a space for comments. The museum educator may want to note an especially enjoyable group, a teacher who might serve on an advisory team, or information that should be emphasized in the future.

Designing a Reservation Form

Design a reservation form that includes all the information you need. Use it every time you are talking with a teacher. It should include the following key points:

1. School/Group Name.
2. Address: Always send a written confirmation. A copy of the reservation form is sufficient and may head off an embarrassing mis-communication.
3. Telephone Number: School numbers are easy to find, but be sure to take numbers from Scout leaders, club organizers, etc. in case of an unexpected change.
4. Contact Person: This should be the person you can call if a problem arises. Often someone other than the teacher calls to make arrangements, but you will need the teacher's name for follow-up.
5. Date of program.
6. Time of program.
7. Length of visit: Be sure to advise the teacher on time considerations such as travel time, time to assemble the group, bathroom visits, and program length. Visits invariably last longer than originally scheduled.
8. Number in group: Students _____ and Chaperones _____.
9. Grade level/Subject area.
10. Program requested: Clearly determine and note the purpose of the visit. This is your best time to communicate about learning needs. How does the trip relate to material being studied? Will it introduce an area of study or perhaps conclude a special unit? What are the teacher's objectives for the trip? Explain how the program works — what kinds of activities are involved, which galleries are visited, what students may need to bring with them. The more clearly you define the students' needs, the more effective your program will be. *Always write down the information discussed to jog your own memory.* It is very easy to forget specifics when you are working with hundreds of children in numerous field trip situations.
11. Admission fees and method of payment: Ask for a check or a single payment. Avoid greeting thirty children, each with a pocketful of change.
12. Special arrangements: Take the initiative in exploring the need for special arrangements. Are there students with disabilities in the group? Is the group staying for lunch? Do they need information about parking or directions to the museum?

Other Useful Ideas

Teacher Open Houses

Many museums find an open house for teachers is an especially useful opportunity for introducing museum programs. Nothing is as effective as a face-to-face sharing of ideas and interests. There is no set format for such a social gathering, but a few hints may be helpful. Teachers have full schedules and may need a few enhancements to attract their interest. Such extras as refreshments, the opportunity to bring family members, and free tickets to a future exhibition, might encourage their attendance. Include lots of handouts and display as many program materials as possible.

Teacher Advisory Committees

Identifying teachers who use the museum especially well can help you form a nucleus of teachers to serve as ongoing advisors and evaluators of new program ideas. Arrange committee meetings and formats to meet teachers' scheduling needs, and always have meaningful agendas. Busy work will quickly diminish your group. Be very clear about what you want from your advisors and give them appropriate credit. An advisory team may function very well as an ad hoc group to be called on for special needs. They assure the teacher input you need and will spread the word within schools about valuable programs. Do not overlook the possibility of including administrators on your advisory team as well. Administrative support is often the key to successful museum-school partnerships.

Field Trip Directories

Many museums have collaborated on field trip directories that provide teachers with program information from museums throughout the region (Philadelphia's *Beyond the Blackboard*, Chester County's *Places of Wonder* and Pittsburgh's *"There's Nothing to Do"*). Although directories are more difficult to keep current, they reach a wide audience and encourage joint programming ideas.

Educator's Pass

An effective way to encourage teachers to become acquainted with your museum and its educational offerings is to make free passes available. Passes can be mailed to teachers or given out on request. They allow the teacher to survey collections and special exhibitions in advance of field trips and create a feeling of good will as well.

Effective partnerships begin with a clear understanding of mutual needs. If museums are to get what we want from schools — an awareness of our goals, preparation for our programs, and an enthusiastic participation at our sites — then we must be certain that our tools of communication are clearly written, thorough and targeted to the right audience. The surest way to avoid the "magical, mystery tour" — the field trip without purpose — is to let teachers know the quality of your exhibitions and programs and the methods that will tie them directly to the school's needs.

References

Donley, Susan K. and Ann Nickerson Kowalski. *"There's Nothing to Do"! A Guide Full of Answers Right in Our Hometown*. Pittsburgh, PA: The Pittsburgh Fund for Arts Education, The Pittsburgh Cultural Trust, 1992.

Sebolt, Alberta. *Collaborative Programs: Museums and Schools*. Sturbridge, MA: Old Sturbridge Village, 1980.

Sheppard, Beverly. *Places of Wonder*. Exton, PA: Chester County Intermediate Unit, 1989.

The Teacher as Partner

Genean Stec

Museum Educator, Chester County Historical Society, and
former Museum Education Coordinator,
Chester County Intermediate Unit

*A major link in the communication between schools and museums
is the classroom teacher. Teachers who are familiar with the museum and museum teaching methods can assure the quality of their
students' experience at our sites. Many museums have developed
teacher training programs and materials to make teachers comfortable in the museum and knowledgeable about its collections.*

*Museums, Magic and Children (1981) cites several reasons to focus
on working directly with teachers. When museum education staff
and docents cannot meet all the requests for service, the well-
trained teacher can develop his/her own programs. Teachers, who
are with their students for a full academic year, can extend the
museum influence longer, and teachers who have participated in
museum training programs can also suggest and help develop new
program ideas.*

*The following chapter details one highly effective teacher-training
program developed in conjunction with an Intermediate Unit in the
state of Pennsylvania. The collaborative project, MEET, and its components suggest a model that could work well for many museum
communities. Variations of the project exist in several areas of the
state. Many other states have comprehensive systems for communicating with teachers and providing in-service training programs. The
author also provides guidelines to using these systems to build relationships between schools and museums.*

Although Chester and Delaware Counties are home to over thirty cultural
institutions, surveys and interviews revealed that few teachers knew about
the wealth of educational materials and programs these institutions had to
offer. Efforts at school/museum networking had been sporadic and short-
lived. The traditional approach to museum education relied on a single, iso-
lated visit that was rarely integrated into the curriculum. Many of the
museums and historic sites in the region were quite small, lacking the
resources to develop, publicize and conduct workshops for teachers, yet they

housed rich collections and experiences for the region's students. The community's wonderful resources were largely unused.

In 1987 a museum educator who had been studying the problem teamed up with the staff of the Chester County Intermediate Unit to design a project to answer the following questions:

- How can teachers be encouraged to use the community's cultural resources?
- How can they gain administrative support for field trips?
- How can museums and schools assure a smooth integration of the field trip into the school curriculum?
- How can museums incorporate the teachers' ideas into future programs?

The project, MEET (Museum Educational Enrichment for Teachers), was developed to address these questions.

MEET was designed as a three-year pilot project funded by a grant from the William Penn Foundation. MEET was unusual because it was not sponsored by a specific museum but was housed in an educational resource center, the Chester County Intermediate Unit. The advantages of the I.U. acting as the sponsoring agent of this project were many.

1. The Chester County Intermediate Unit was a neutral organization that already served to collaborate educational programs.
2. Its administrative structure gave stability and credibility to the project coordinator's position and to MEET's projects.
3. The I.U. provided a centralized distribution point for all program information using existing administrative and communicative channels to the schools.
4. The I.U. could award continuing education credits and master's equivalency credits through its well-established in-service program.

MEET employed a project coordinator to act as a liaison between museums and schools, encouraging dialogue and facilitating the development of new programs. The coordinator got "the ball rolling"; she provided an extra pair of hands, additional staff, energy and often clout to get projects done in a timely manner. She was also an advocate of both teachers and museum educators, possessing the objectivity to address their separate needs. In addition, the project coordinator assembled an advisory committee which included school administrators as well as teachers and museum representatives.

A key to MEET's operation was that it did not dictate the content of museum programs. MEET encouraged museums to use their individual strengths as the basis for educational programming. Some collaborative projects assign each participant a specific role to play; MEET sought only to coordinate the goals each museum set for itself. Similarly, the project encouraged teachers to use museums in a range of interdisciplinary activities. MEET was established as an organizing tool to encourage productive and ongoing interaction between museums and schools.

The first MEET project was the creation of a directory of local cultural institutions. *Places of Wonder: A Teacher's Field Trip Guide to Cultural Institutions in Chester and Delaware Counties* contains a concise description of twenty-seven cultural institutions and the school programs they offer. It also includes pertinent information on the planning and implementation of effective field trips. The guide was distributed free of charge to all schools in Chester and Delaware Counties, with one copy sent to the school librarian and another to the assistant principal or curriculum coordinator. In addition, special workshops were held at central locations in both counties to introduce the MEET project and the guide to school principals. Each attendee was given two copies, one for himself and one for a teacher of his choice.

Guidelines to Developing Resource Directories

The following guidelines, learned during the MEET experience, may assist others in developing a regional museum directory.

1. Begin by holding a meeting with local museum educators to discuss the project and plan a format. Design a form to collect the agreed-upon information that will be included in the book. Design the form to be as close as possible to the planned page layout.

2. Determine the project's budget and how it will be financed. Designate a project coordinator and determine if that position will be staffed by paid or volunteer personnel.

3. Plan the distribution of the directory. Will it be given away? sold? a combination of both? Who will handle the sales and distribution? How will it be advertised? How many copies will be printed? Where will they be stored? Will this be an annual project? How will revisions and additions be made? Each of these questions will impact the format and design of the project.

4. To collect the information for the directory, mail a questionnaire to each cultural institution with a self-addressed, stamped envelope and a noted deadline. Follow the mailing with a telephone call to encourage participation and adherence to the deadline.

5. To secure funding, approach local businesses, the chamber of commerce, the local tourist information office or investigate foundation or corporate grant support.

6. Develop a comprehensive mailing list. Include: public, private and parochial school libraries, community libraries, curriculum directors, teachers, department chairpersons, principals, leaders of scout programs, day care directors and after school program coordinators.

In-Service Opportunities and Teacher Training

A major component of the MEET project was the development of in-service workshops for teachers. The goals of these workshops were:

- to expand teachers' awareness of the educational opportunities available in regional museums;
- to bring teachers to the sites and familiarize them with the nature of object-based learning;
- to train teachers to use the museum and its resources to their fullest extent;
- to encourage teachers to share and develop ideas for new museum education experiences.

A strong motivating factor for teachers to participate in the in-service programs was the opportunity to earn credits toward salary track advancement and permanent certification. All in-service courses offered by state Intermediate Units must be approved through application to the Pennsylvania Department of Education as well as by each district Intermediate Unit. One in-service credit equals fifteen hours of class time. Each school district sets its own policy concerning the benefits derived from taking in-service courses. This is often part of the teachers' contract negotiations. Contact your district Intermediate Unit for more information.

The MEET in-service courses are publicized through a fall, spring and summer in-service course brochure that is distributed to all curriculum directors and schools in the county.

The following is a sampling of some of the most successful in-service courses offered through MEET.

Beyond the Classroom: The Successful Field Trip

A summer in-service program
Monday-Friday from 9:30 a.m. to 4:00 p.m.
2 in-service credits; 30 class hours
Collaborative effort of more than eight museums
Class enrollment limited to 25

Beyond the Classroom introduces teachers to a variety of sites, programs, and object-based teaching methods. The course teaches specific methods for conducting successful field trips by example throughout the session. Teachers receive behind-the-scenes tours of each museum, become acquainted with the programs, workshops and special events available to teachers and students, learn the mechanics of arranging group visits, and sample program activities.

Beyond the Classroom presents theories in the study of material culture and techniques employed in hands-on investigation. Teachers have practical experience observing, planning, and evaluating the field trips taken during the course. Participants explore the learning potential of such sites as an eighteenth-century industrial complex, a Revolutionary War battlefield, a regional art museum, a research library, a historic house museum, and a nature and environmental center. Group discussions are planned throughout the course to encourage the sharing of ideas and observations among the teachers and museum educators.

At the conclusion of the course, teachers present a field trip experience they have designed for the students they teach, using one of the museums as their destination. This final project includes the development of pre-visit materials, site activities and classroom follow-up, along with formal and informal evaluation of the experience by both students and teachers.

Encourage, Explore and Appreciate: Art in the Brandywine Valley

A summer or Saturday in-service program
Monday-Friday, half days, or five Saturdays, half days
1 in-service credit; 15 class hours
Collaborative effort of five museums
Class enrollment limited to 25

Five Brandywine Valley art institutions combine to demonstrate the rich and diverse methods of teaching art and art appreciation both in and out of the classroom. Teaching methods include the use of authentic art objects and museum quality reproductions along with a variety of written materials. The five institutions present observation and study skills that work with collections in the fine arts, regional crafts, decorative arts and architecture and emphasize how to relate art to the curriculum. Opportunities are frequent for interaction between teachers and museum educators that can add to existing museum programs.

Chester County Rediscovered:
Teaching Local History in and Out of the Classroom

A summer or Saturday in-service program
Monday-Friday, half days, or five Saturdays, half days
1 in-service credit; 15 class hours
Collaborative effort of six museums
Class enrollment limited to 25

A historical society, archives, nature center, two historic house museums and an outdoor historic industrial complex coordinate a series of visits that demonstrate methods of teaching local history both in and out of the classroom. Teaching methods include the use of oral, material, cultural and natural history. One session combines a lecture and field exploration on the unique relationship between geology and the history of Chester County. Another introduces techniques used in conducting archival research and studying primary

sources. Through hands-on investigation and role-playing, participants explore a variety of ways to study objects and artifacts that are a part of local history. Once again, interaction between teachers and museum educators is stressed.

Museum Education Internship: Working Behind the Scenes in a Museum

Summer in-service program
Monday-Friday, half days or full days
4 in-service credits; 60 class hours
All museums may participate
Enrollment limited to number of approved projects

One of the most successful and popular of the summer in-service programs, this course offers teachers the opportunity to work directly with museum staffs on specific educational projects. The course familiarizes teachers with museum collections and educational methods and involves them in in-depth museum research and program development. The research collected is used to enhance and/or develop new museum programs for students and teachers. Teachers work with a variety of museum staff, learning behind-the-scenes collections care, research methods, exhibition development approaches, and integration of collections into educational programs. All projects are closely supervised by the MEET project coordinator. At the conclusion of the internship, teachers are required to submit a five-page summary paper describing their internship experiences and how they will impact their classroom teaching.

Teacher Workshops

During the three-year grant period MEET conducted several day-long workshops for teachers and school administrators. Like the in-service courses, the workshops utilized the expertise of museum educators and collections of their museums. Among the programs presented were:

Stimulating Creative Thinking Through the Visual Arts

This workshop was designed for art teachers and teachers of the gifted. It used the resources of the Brandywine River Museum and the Delaware Art Museum as a springboard for the enhancement of creative thinking skills. The workshop format included a lecture and teaching demonstration followed by hands-on activities in the galleries which applied the teaching techniques presented in the morning session. All teachers visited both sites.

Teaching History With Style

This day-long program was designed for teachers at both the primary and the secondary level. Drawing on the resources of several historic sites, the program opened with a lecture on the use of material culture in teaching.

Collections were used to demonstrate research skills and the development of inductive thinking skills. Practical suggestions on ways to involve students in participation in History Day were also included.

Celebrating Earth Day

This day-long workshop was presented for elementary school teachers. The workshop focused on the environmental issues surrounding water, open space and the wetlands in Chester County. Teachers participated in hands-on activities at a regional environmental center which could be easily duplicated in the classroom and at the other nature and environmental sites throughout the county.

Learning in the Third Dimension:
Object-Based Teaching Techniques for the Classroom

The workshop, which met at a decorative arts museum, focused on American material culture and how to use object-based learning techniques to teach the humanities. Using the decorative arts collections as a learning laboratory, teachers explored effective ways of using objects from the past in history, language arts and fine arts curriculum units.

Curriculum Directors' Workshop

To begin spreading the word about MEET, a day-long workshop was designed for curriculum directors in Chester and Delaware Counties. The workshop provided examples of the services and resources offered by MEET and included two visits to cultural institutions where presentations involved the attendees in participatory activities and discussion.

Teacher workshops offer unique opportunities to share ideas, interests and new program materials.

29

Creating Successful In-Service Courses and Workshops

The following guidelines for creating in-service programs and workshops for teachers were developed through the MEET project. They would be equally appropriate for any individual museum planning such learning opportunities.

■ Begin by meeting with the school administrator who handles the in-service course program for your county's Intermediate Unit or school districts. Be organized and present well-developed ideas for your programs.

■ Establish joint goals and objectives with school administrators.

■ Stress the working partnership between museums and schools. Relate all the activities and materials to the curriculum.

■ Target in-service programs to address primary, intermediate and upper elementary and high school groups.

■ Always include hands-on activities and handouts.

■ Vary the pace of the program. Do not lecture to teachers...involve them in discussions. Remember, teachers learn as they were taught.

■ Involve as many people from the museum staff as possible: curators, archivists, librarians, registrars, educators, even the director if possible.

■ Develop collaborative programs combining the strengths of one institution with those of another.

■ Use the teachers' language. Be familiar with the rudiments of writing lesson plans and curriculum objectives.

■ Sessions should be humanly paced — no more than two hours without a break. A comfortable setting and refreshments add a welcoming touch to the program and to the museum's image.

■ Flexibility is key.

■ Remember, it is better to leave teachers with a feeling of wanting more than to overload them.

■ Evaluation is an important component. Evaluate each program formally (questionnaire) and informally (staff observations). Then act on the information gathered.

MEET Teaching Materials

MEET also coordinated the development of teaching materials that would extend the life of the project. MEET provided the financial resources and the staff to coordinate the production of several traveling trunks. These were made available at no cost to teachers for classroom use and could be borrowed for up to two weeks. The scheduling, delivery and pick-up of the trunks was handled through the MEET coordinator, using the Intermediate Unit's delivery system. The trunks used reproductions of artifacts and primary sources to teach about such topics as the Battle of the Brandywine, Native Americans in the Delaware Valley and the Civil War experience in Chester County.

The trunks represent a first step toward the development of a teacher resource center as a component of MEET. Although the original funding has expired, the project has shifted to the Education Department of the Chester County Historical Society. In-service credits and the use of the Intermediate Unit's mailing system will continue as MEET enters a new phase of its service to area museums and schools.

Learning Theories in the Museum Setting

Inez S. Wolins, Ph.D.

Director, Wichita (Kansas) Art Museum, and
former Curator of Education,
Pennsylvania Academy of the Fine Arts

While director of The Children's Museum in Boston, Michael Spock described learning in a museum as "landmark learning." Not every child will have the same experience, but each may be moved in a special, personal way by something he or she encounters. That discovery may become a "landmark" in the child's lifelong learning experience.

The informal nature of a museum setting provides a unique opportunity to address the individual learning styles of each child. Educational psychologists have only recently begun to appreciate how different people are in their learning styles. They bring different kinds of skills, "intelligences," motivations and experiences to each learning experience. Museum environments contrast with the more formal and structured classroom environment and invite a variety of approaches to learning.

The museum-school partnership should develop the opportunities present in the more open atmosphere of a museum. In this chapter, Inez Wolins explores current theories about learning and their specific applications to the museum setting.

"**F**rom the beginning of life, the inward flow of sensations and experiences is organized by the brain in a variety of ways. Preference to learn by touch, by vision, or by language is developed by children and young adults in the course of sustained inquiries, and from there emerges a reliance upon a particular way of learning." (John-Steiner, 1985)

Researcher and psychologist Howard Gardner (1991) wishes that we could make schools more like museums. He imagines an educational environment in which children take "courses" in their local children's or science museum. They would apprentice with knowledgeable adults and other students.

When students are exposed to a more knowledgeable guide who demonstrates the way to use a skill or solve a problem, educators call this an example of mental modelling (Gentner and Stevens, 1983). Museums are great

places to illustrate this concept, whether the skill is butter-churning, using a farm tool, "reading" a work of art, or testing some hypothesis. Gardner (1991) contrasts schools, which connote serious, regular, formal, deliberately decontextualizing and compartmentalizing learning, with museums — institutions which he feels are casual, entertaining and enjoyable.

Science and children's museums, according to Gardner (1991), have exhibits and activities and role models to motivate students, whereas schools seem to rely on modes of learning through reading, lectures about remote subjects, and tests based on drill-and-practice of memory of disconnected facts. The difference between the two environments is fairly obvious — to Gardner, museums represent places filled with activity, experience, open-ended choices and opportunities, informality, and wonder. They are concept-centered or experience-based and are more likely to meet the needs of children to learn through activity.

Not all museum experiences are as ideal as those described by Gardner, however. A student's experience in collection-based museums — especially those containing works of art and historical objects and artifacts — is often very different. It is frequently more like a school experience, but it doesn't have to be. What would it mean if we could transform museums into environments for open-ended, self-directed, apprenticeship experiences, filled with dynamic projects based on the evocative content of collections? Some museum education departments are doing just this and successfully engaging students in very meaningful and creative ways.

The educators in these museums acknowledge that learning is an active process. It involves making sense of and organizing the information we perceive from the world around us and from what we already know of the world. Children come to build a foundation or knowledge base as they grow and develop over time. When these youngsters visit our museums, they come with a range of knowledge and experiences, and they come with their own preferences for learning. Learning happens for children in different ways, so it is important to structure a range of opportunities to help children learn in ways that match their preferences.

Learning is a natural and never-ending process. Yet, learning is idiosyncratic. We learn in ways unique to ourselves. We process information in different ways. Researchers are continually challenged to find out more about this issue of how we learn, think and remember.

Harvard education professor Bernice McCarthy (1980), for example, has even created different categorical labels for types of learners. Here are some examples of her work:

Innovative Learners

seek personal meaning
are divergent thinkers
believe in their own experiences
are idea people

Analytic Learners

seek facts
learn by thinking through ideas
need to know what experts think

Common Sense Learners

seek usability
need to know how things work
seek hands-on experiences
deal with practical application

Dynamic Learners

seek hidden possibilities
learn by self-discovery
are risk-takers
seek action

These learning styles are very generalized categories. People do not fit neatly into one category or the other. We are composites of all those types, depending on two variables: 1) the task to be learned and 2) the physical and social context in which we are learning something. In different situations we might lean more towards one style or another. If we can become sensitive to our personal approaches to learning, then we have a greater chance of being aware of our visitors' needs as learners. Our styles of learning strongly influence how we teach in museums and how we design exhibits.

Think about your own learning style. Select a skill from the following list.

Swimming (or any sport)
Cooking
Knitting
Any sort of craft or building task
Playing chess
Driving a car
Giving a museum tour
Playing the piano or any instrument
Gardening/flower arranging

How would you go about learning one of the above skills? For example, in learning to swim, someone might have started by playing in the water, or by watching an older sibling, or by taking lessons at camp, or by starting in the shallow end with a parent practicing how to blow bubbles. That complex skill — learning to swim — was broken down into smaller parts, and the individual parts were mastered before moving on to breathing, harder strokes or deeper water. The notion of mastery of a complex skill has been explored in museum education as well (Wolins, 1990).

Now, enter a gallery in your museum and determine how each of the learners described in the categories above might react to one of the objects she sees. What kinds of questions might he ask? What kinds of teaching techniques would interest each learner? Formulate an approach to teaching with these objects geared toward each learning style or consider redesigning an existing exhibition with each of these learners in mind. Learners of all types will be taking tours and viewing exhibitions, so our goal should be to balance our teaching or exhibition design to reach each learner.

Howard Gardner (1983), like McCarthy, also believes that students have preferences or styles of learning, and that from birth, students possess multiple intelligences. He claims that all students will have strengths in more than one intelligence, with one or two areas dominating. Educational researcher Lynn Dierking (1991) has classified some of Gardner's work this way:

Linguistic/verbal intelligence

A child who is highly verbal, likes to read and write, and has a
good memory for names, places, dates and fact

Logical-mathematical intelligence

A child who enjoys math, and who likes to play
(and often wins at) chess or other games of strategy

Spatial intelligence

A child who has good visual memory, can easily read charts,
graphs, and maps and likes watching movies, slides
or looking at photographs

Musical intelligence

A child who plays an instrument, remembers songs, and says
he needs to hear music to concentrate

Bodily-kinesthetic intelligence

A child who performs well in competitive sports,
likes physical activities and demonstrating skills like crafts

Interpersonal intelligence

A child who has many friends, likes to socialize and
enjoys playing games in groups

Intrapersonal intelligence

A child who prefers to be alone when she pursues projects
and is motivated to complete projects independently

Return to a museum gallery thinking about a specific child you know and consider which works of art or historic artifacts that child might prefer, as well as ways to help the child look at, think about, and respond to other objects on exhibit. Consider what it might take to motivate the child. This gives us an idea of the complexity and challenges of the teaching role in a museum.

Motivating Students to Learn in Museums: A Theory of Learning From Social Interaction

The Russian psychologist Lev Vygotsky (1978) conducted pioneering research in cognition, grounded in the study of its social origins. Cognition encompasses all of the processes by which we gain knowledge of the world — thinking, remembering, learning, perceiving and understanding. Vygotsky's work applies especially well to what we do in museums because the nature of the students' visit to the museum is built largely upon social experiences for the children. Teachers and museum educators may differ in their goals for visiting a museum, but for students, the trip deviates from the routine of the school day and is very much a social event (Wolins, 1991).

Vygotsky (1978) was principally interested in the social foundations of cognition and the importance of instruction in development. For him, instruction always resulted from a social relationship between individuals. The nature of social interaction is an important variable in the learning process. In a Vygotskian framework, social interaction focuses on intellectual content; when confronted with a concept to teach or a problem to solve, the knowledge or skill of the teacher or another student in the group influences the roles each will take toward others.

It has long been understood in the field of education that adult role models have a profound influence over the development and learning of children (Vygotsky, 1978; Bigge, 1982). Research has shown that the involvement of adults in informal learning situations actually improved learning (Forman, 1987; Rogoff, 1990). This theory suggests that museum educators should create strategies to help teachers own parts of the museum lesson, since they are better able to extend the museum experience back in the classroom. We also should not forget about the other adults who accompany children on school field trips; they could be enlisted to lead small groups, guide a discussion or conduct an activity, if properly instructed to do so.

Personal Investment in the Learning Process

Learning is a function of the amount of invested mental effort involved in processing material (Salomon, 1981). In order for children to learn in museum settings, they must make personal investments in the process of learning. Mental investment is an active and involving process which requires students to be motivated (Malone and Lepper, 1987).

One of the most prevalent ways to help students become motivated in the museum is through participation with materials that offer challenges. This can be translated into the agenda for the design of instructional materials for students to use in museum environments; learners will select those materials which arouse their curiosity and spark their motivation to explore further.

Pre-schoolers at the Pennsylvania Academy of the Fine Arts Museum use role-playing activities to "de-code" the subjects, activities, and emotional responses of American paintings.

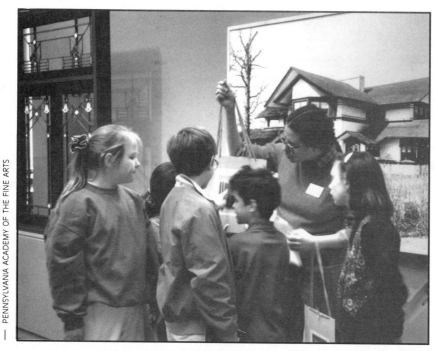

Students can be instructed to work in pairs or smaller groups to ensure greater participation during museum visits.

These materials may include age-appropriate worksheets, grab bags, gallery activity kits, handling objects in a study collection, drawing, writing, storytelling, or role-playing. The act of participating with these materials gets students involved in their own learning and demands mental investment.

Effectively designed lesson plans for students which incorporate materials and activities for use in the galleries (versus lecture tours) can encourage learners to grasp new concepts quickly, relate them to past shared experiences and knowledge, integrate information with previous knowledge, and retain in memory for later application.

For example, at the Pennsylvania Academy of the Fine Arts Museum,

PENNSYLVANIA ACADEMY OF THE FINE ARTS

PENNSYLVANIA ACADEMY OF THE FINE ARTS

school groups usually arrive on a bus which seats close to sixty students. Teachers are asked to divide the children into four equal groups. Four volunteer docents and/or teaching interns from the Pennsylvania Academy of the Fine Arts School conduct the museum lessons. Thus, the ratio between museum teacher and students is usually less than one to fifteen. The smaller group size encourages greater participation from students during their visit.

Lessons incorporate a variety of learning activities. The first photograph illustrates a pre-school class in a gallery devoted to nineteenth-century American genre paintings. The classroom teacher selects two students who use props and costumes similar to those found in a nearby painting. Dressed in character, children choose a question from the picnic basket, and the docent or teacher reads it aloud. The costumed children answer the question by looking at the painting. Questions might include:

Where are you going dressed like that? Why don't you go to work? What time of day is it? What are you doing? By hearing questions asked and answered, children then make up some questions of their own, exploring the work of art through active inquiry and critical thinking skills.

PENNSYLVANIA ACADEMY OF THE FINE ARTS

After studying symmetry and architectural floorplans and elevations, students work in teams to search for and sketch details found in the museum's building.

In another photograph, older students in a decorative arts exhibition work in pairs. Students wear picture cards on their backs, and one asks the other a series of yes/no questions trying to identify the object on the card with the original in the gallery. After both objects are found, the pair join together to complete a worksheet about the form and function of the objects, their use in context, and the architect's intent in their creation.

During a lesson about the museum's Victorian gothic building, a team learns how to decode a floorplan. They study symmetry and ornamentation before finding and sketching examples of ornamental design inspired by nature. They return to the group to share their findings and are led into a

lively debate comparing Victorian style and taste with architecture built in their own lifetime.

In the final photograph, a group of elementary-aged students select a toy animal from a bag. The animal becomes the springboard for discussion about a painting of Noah and his ark. The museum teacher takes the facilitator's role and asks open-ended questions to elicit multiple responses from the group. Questions include: What is special about your animal? Where is it located in the painting? How is your animal different from the animal in the painting? What would it have been like to be on that ark for forty days and forty nights? Students participate in this introductory activity before moving to another gallery where they create and share stories based on individually selected nineteenth-century American narrative paintings.

The examples above demonstrate that museums can be models of institutions where students encounter a variety of learning opportunities to enhance school-based learning. In museums, students can try activities on their own or in small groups, watch a demonstration, apply a concept through guided experimentation, listen to an explainer, see a short film, participate in a debate. When student-directed activities are combined with teacher-directed experiences for individual learners, pairs, small groups, teams and entire classes, educators shift their roles from dispensers of information to designers of rich and varied learning environments for children.

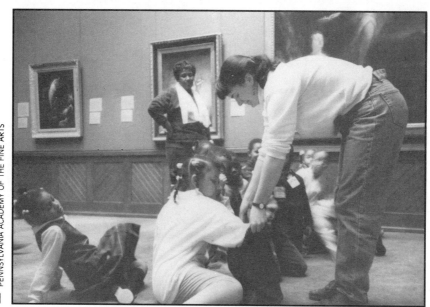

— PENNSYLVANIA ACADEMY OF THE FINE ARTS

Props, study collection objects, and hands-on materials enable a diversity of learners to make meaning in the museum.

Observing Students During a Structured Visit to Your Museum

Use the following guidelines to assess the educational experiences of student groups in your museum and to reflect about how to construct engaging ways for students to learn during their visit.

Select a class to watch and use the questions below as a guide to assessing the experiences of students.

1. What was the docent's/instructor's objective in this program/lecture/tour? Was it achieved?

2. Describe the program briefly: Collection or exhibit used, sequence of activities, discussion, materials, etc.

3. Notice the role of the museum docent or instructor: What kind of relationship did the instructor establish with the children? adults? What kinds of questions were asked? In what ways did the instructor respond to the answers? How did the instructor involve the children with the objects?

4. Observe the response of the class: What kinds of behavior indicated the children's level (or lack) of interest at different points in the program/tour? What were the most successful parts of the program, based on the children's responses? Adults' responses? Was the program appropriate to the interests and abilities of the class?

5. What role did the teacher assume during the visit? What was the effect, if any, on the children and the program? What were the teacher's goals or agendas at the museum? How could you tell?

6. Based on the above, what (if anything) would you have changed in this program? Why?

7. What did you learn about school visits in museums that would be useful to you in planning your next program? How will you prepare the museum docents/instructors to conduct the program?

References

Bigge, M. *Learning Theories for Teachers*. New York: Harper and Row, 1982.

Dierking, L. and Springuel, M. (eds.). "Current Issues in Museum Learning." *The Journal of Museum Education,*16. Winter, 1991.

Forman, E.A. "Learning Through Peer Interaction: A Vygotskian Perspective." *Genetic Epistemologist*, 15, 1987, 6-15.

Gardner, H. *Frames of Mind: Multiple Intelligences*. New York: Basic Books, 1983.

Gardner, H. "Making Schools More Like Museums." *Education Week*, 40, October 9, 1991.

Gentner, D. and Stevens, A.L. (eds.). *Mental Models*. Hillsdale, NJ: Eribaum Associates, 1983.

John-Steiner, V. *Notebooks of the Mind: Explorations of Thinking*. New York: Harper and Row, 1985.

Malone, T.W. and Lepper, M.R. "Making Learning Fun: A Taxonomic Model of Intrinsic Motivation for Learning." In R.E. Snow and M.J. Farr (eds.). *Aptitude, Learning and Instruction III: Cognitive and Affective Process Analysis*, 1987, pp. 223-253.

McCarthy, B. *The 4-Mat System: Teaching to Learning Styles and Right/Left Mode Techniques*. Barrington, IL: Excel, Inc., 1980.

Rogoff, B. *Apprenticeship in Thinking*. New York: Oxford University Press, 1990.

Ross, J.A. and Raphael, D. "Communication and Problem Solving Achievement in Cooperative Learning Groups." *Journal of Curriculum Studies*, March/April, 1990, pp. 149-164.

Salomon, G. *Communication and Education: Social and Psychological Interactions*. Beverly Hills: Sage Publications, 1981.

Vygotsky, L.S. *Mind in Society: The Development of Higher Psychological Processes*. Cambridge, MA; Harvard University Press, 1978.

Williams, P. "Object-oriented Learning in Art Museums." *The Journal of Museum Education*, 7 (2), 1982, pp. 12-15.

Wolins, I.S. "Teaching the Teachers." *Museum News*, May/June, 1990, pp. 71-75.

Wolins, I. "Children's Memories for Museum Visits: A Qualitative Study." Paper presented at the 86th Annual Meeting of the American Association of Museums, Denver, CO, 1991.

The author gratefully acknowledges input for this chapter from Pennsylvania Academy museum educators Judy Ringold, Tamsin Wolff and Anne Martin.

Aspects of a Successful Field Trip

Beverly Sheppard

The school field trip is the heart of the museum education experience. When the bus unloads and a parade of students climbs the front steps to the museum, anticipation is high. A well-planned, clearly focused field trip — one that reflects the partnership of school and museum — will reward the expectations of students, teachers and museum educators alike.

Learning in a museum is not automatic. The field trip objectives will compete with the novelty of the setting, the anxiety of the visitors, the social opportunities of a day out of school and the variables of personality and experience. They will be altered by the participation of the teacher, the preparation of the students and the plan for the day. The successful field trip is a balanced mix of ingredients that acknowledges the students' varied needs within a thoughtful, focused set of activities.

This chapter defines the nature of a focused field trip and its components; it outlines the three-part structure that ensures the close relationship of the museum experience to the classroom curriculum. The following chapter will illustrate techniques for providing interactive experiences in the galleries.

My sister and I grew up in the Cleveland Museum of Art. Every Saturday after art class, we played a game in the galleries. We would each pick out our favorite object and then present it to one another as "my painting," telling why we liked it and sometimes even becoming the artist, explaining how we painted it. We started this game in the armor exhibit, describing to one another which suit of armor we would wear, how we would put it on and what battles we would fight. Gradually our tastes became more sophisticated, and we moved on to many schools of painting.

Although to us it was a game to play while we waited for our ride home, it initiated a lifelong learning style. We focused our attention on one section of the museum each week, taking home with us a vibrant image of at least one wonderful work of art. We couldn't wait to go back the following week for a new adventure. To us, the museum was a magical place. Like a library, it offered endless discoveries to return to again and again.

Focusing a field trip for your student visitors creates the comparison between museums and libraries. It acknowledges the myriad of learning

experiences within the museum's collection, illustrating how the museum is a resource to be returned to over and over. It also demonstrates how students can learn from selected objects, applying observation and thinking skills. The focused field trip is not the "grand tour"; it is a field trip with a specific theme and a set of defined learning objectives.

The Field Museum of Natural History publication, *Teach the Mind, Touch the Spirit* states,

> "Class field trips in which students trek from exhibit to exhibit, take a quick look and move on to the next, may be likened to flipping through the pages of a book. With limited involvement and only chance relationships to school studies, such field trips only begin to touch the potential of museums as learning environments. *Focused* field trips are a powerfully effective alternative."
> (Voris, Sedzielarz, Blackmon, 1986, p.3)

Focus is a theme. A focused field trip is a learning experience planned around a central learning purpose and a set of clear learning objectives. The focus of a field trip will encourage many uses for one collection. One group of students, for example, may view a decorative arts collection to learn about woodworking and joinery techniques. Another might use the same collection to learn about lifestyles in a specific period of history. A student group might select only the chairs from several periods to demonstrate concepts of style and elaboration. Or, the entire gallery might be the setting for a seek-and-find game, looking for animal images in the decorative arts.

Building a field trip around a distinctive theme offers several clear advantages.

1. The theme allows the museum staff to plan as educators, identifying and defining specific learning objectives and selecting the most appropriate exhibits and teaching methods to achieve each objective. A focused field trip gives the museum educator the best opportunity to apply object-based teaching skills and to plan questioning strategies.
2. The theme and focus allow the museum educators to target specific age groups and age-appropriate learning skills.
3. The theme enhances school-museum communication. The school visit is not just a "trip to the museum"; it is a trip to "learn about colonial clothing and how it was made." The focus is the key to integrating the visit with the curriculum, and it clarifies expectations on both sides.
4. The theme elicits more enthusiastic administrative support. The field trip is not seen as just a day off but as a valid educational experience. The field trip is not mayhem, but an integrated part of a structured curriculum.
5. The theme assists both teacher and museum educator in determining activities for pre-visit preparation and post-visit follow-up.

The pre-trip, trip, and post-trip activities have a better shot at being developed as an integrated set of learning experiences.

6. A thematic approach encourages an interdisciplinary use of museum collections. For example, a group of English teachers visited the Delaware Museum of Art to focus on the Pre-Raphaelite painting collection to learn about symbolism in Victorian culture, linking art and literature. Science teachers used a historic mill site to teach about simple machines.

Before and After: Two Facets of a Field Trip

PRE-TRIP ACTIVITIES

Pre-trip activities set the learning stage for the museum visit and prepare students both emotionally and intellectually. Although many teachers will prepare the students very effectively on their own, others will require some help from you. Before sending pre-trip suggestions to the teacher, introduce them during your initial phone call. That first conversation may convince teachers of the effectiveness of careful trip preparation.

Pre-trip activities should accomplish two goals: 1) introduce the museum and set expectations for the visit and 2) introduce the subject matter and object-based teaching methods. Introducing the museum will reduce the novelty and anxiety that can distract students from the learning activities you have carefully planned. Research has shown that providing pre-trip preparation has consistently enhanced the learning that takes place during the visit (Falk, Dierking, 1992).

Pre-trip suggestions may be included in a simple letter to the teacher, or they may be more elaborate, using slides, worksheets, even an orientation visit by a museum educator. A letter can encourage teachers to prepare their students with a class discussion about the museum visit. What do they expect to see? What other museums have they visited? What did they like best? Students can share their own collections and discuss how they take care of them. Concerns for collections can introduce rules about not touching and explain them as well. If possible, include a picture of your museum, slides of collections, a museum brochure with pictures or perhaps a simple worksheet that illustrates some things the children will see. Although a degree of novelty enhances learning, a totally unfamiliar environment will distract students from your learning goals.

The goal of pre-trip activities is to help students make clear connections between what they are studying in the classroom and what they will encounter in the museum. Since much classroom teaching is based on reading and listening skills, and museum teaching uses perceptual and observational skills, students should be prepared for the difference. Provide ideas to

the teacher to help develop perceptual skills. Students might play games that require matching and classification skills, mystery objects, or physical descriptions, like "I Spy." Students could bring objects from home for a mini-museum activity to study display techniques, appropriate rules, and observation skills. The museum might also provide postcards of objects with directions for an inquiry lesson.

Close integration with curriculum should ensure preparation for the topic of the museum visit. The museum can also help by sending a list of such things as key vocabulary words, new concepts, maps, appropriate research topics, as well as worksheets, reproduction artifacts, or even a museum speaker. Many museums use outreach kits of objects as an orientation to a museum lesson.

POST-TRIP FOLLOW-UP

The museum experience and the excitement it generates need to be reinforced. Post-trip activities build on the students' learning and enthusiasm and should be encouraged. As with pre-trip preparation, many teachers will generate post-trip activities on their own. Others, however, will benefit from your ideas. The ideal museum-school partnership will encourage joint planning of these experiences.

A simple printed sheet handed to the teacher at the close of the visit can encourage follow-up. Suggest two kinds of follow-up activities: a review of the information learned and a creative interpretation of the material. Reinforce important vocabulary and concepts. Provide a review sheet of key ideas. If students did worksheets or any kind of written activity in the museum, ask teachers to go over them with the students. What did they enjoy the most? What was most surprising? What new information did they learn? What did they notice that was not on the worksheet? What related to something they learned in

An exhibit of student-built projects culminates a series of programs on early life in Chester County.

the classroom? Many teachers ask students to write thank you letters to the museum. Encourage them to expand the letter into including the student's favorite experience or most startling observation. These letters also assist museum educators with evaluation.

Turn student observations into creative projects such as dioramas, posters, diaries, bulletin boards or various arts and crafts. One enterprising class followed up an architectural walking tour with "travel brochures," highlighting the town's attractions. Another class developed a townscape from shoe boxes and arranged an exhibit and parents' reception at the host museum. Creative activities such as developing a museum game, writing a short story based on the visit (e.g., "If I lived in 1750...") or writing a skit, have the advantage of allowing an open-ended interpretation and reinforcing the individual nature of a museum encounter.

Along with encouraging follow-up activities, also ask teachers and students to evaluate their trip. Prepare a simple evaluation form that can be done quickly, but that also leaves room for extended answers if teachers would like to elaborate. Refer to your pre-established learning goals as the key to your evaluation. Did you achieve them? List each goal with a range of responses from high to low for the simplest objective response.

An evaluation form also allows you to check on logistical questions. Could everyone see? hear? move freely through the galleries? Were your pre-trip materials adequate? Were there unexpected logistical problems — problems parking? finding the building? Encourage teachers to solicit responses from their students as well — perhaps filling out the form together or at least discussing its contents. Chaperones also should be asked about their experiences.

The evaluation should be a two-way process. In a partnership, both schools and museums have obligations to the success of the trip. Museum teachers should also keep a journal of their experiences, noting such things as which teachers brought well-prepared classes, what groups exhibited discipline problems, who developed interesting follow-up ideas, and other observations about each class. This information provides guidelines for return visits and can be acted upon the following year.

The Museum Visit

Learning is an active process. Learning in a museum is a process that involves looking, questioning, examining, comparing, analyzing, hypothesizing, and evaluating. The special contribution of museums to the educational experience is the emphasis on perceptual skills — learning based on an encounter with objects. *Keeping the objects in your collection as the primary means of communication is the single most important factor in presenting a museum learning experience.*

The focus of the museum field trip establishes the learning objectives. The museum educator then must plan the collections and methods that best fulfill these objectives. **Remember, don't do things in the museum that could be done just as well in school.** Keep in mind also that learning is a social activity. Students on a field trip will have a social agenda of their own. You can facilitate their learning by accepting this aspect of the visit and planning activities that can be done in pairs, in small groups and in the larger group setting.

The best teaching method for real learning and enjoyment in the museum setting is an interactive one. Some museums will permit "hands-on" activities, allowing students to experience the tactile qualities of texture, weight, size, shape and construction. "Hands-on" involves many senses and allows a variety of learning methods. It is the most direct encounter possible with the "real stuff" of the museum.

Not all museums, however, can permit the handling of objects in their care. Similar, less valuable objects may be substituted and reproduction objects can simulate the real experience. The difference between the real and the reproduction, however, must be clarified to avoid creating a confusion about what can and cannot be touched. Students should also be taught the reasons behind "Don't touch" and be made a part of the museum team that preserves objects for the future.

Elaboration in design is the theme pursued by this student at Chester County Historical Society. A museum-designed worksheet encourages his close observation of details.

There are many excellent interactive methods that do not require the actual touching of objects. One key technique is the use of skillful questioning. Good questioning techniques encourage students to do their own thinking and analysis while the museum teacher helps to focus their inquiry. This kind of learning is child-centered, based on the student's activity and

Writing Effective Questions

There are many excellent books that outline good questioning techniques, including *The Good Guide* (1986) and *Creative Museum Methods and Educational Techniques* (1982). The following general guidelines are useful in preparing a program that emphasizes discovery as a key to learning.

1. **Questions should be carefully planned.** Learning moves from the concrete to the abstract. It builds on what one already knows to permit new associations, to rearrange facts and to see new relationships. Questions should be planned sequentially. A range of question types are defined in numbers four through seven below.

2. **Questions should be directed toward the learning objectives of the field trip.** What should students know when the field trip is over? What further inquiry do you want to stimulate? Plan your questions to meet these specific goals.

3. **Questions should lead from the simple to the complex, the specific to the abstract.** Asking a group to comment about the furniture style in a room may be too general. Focus their attention first on the specific features — the shapes in the design, the configuration of the feet, the curve of the arms. By encouraging observation and comparison, you can lead students to an understanding of the broader concepts.

4. **Questions should promote looking.** Focus on observation, details and comparisons. What shapes do you see in this painting? How does this chair foot differ from the one next to it?

5. **Questions should encourage the integration of new information.** How do you think this was made? What problems would you have using it?

6. **Questions should encourage interest and creative thinking.** What other designs could they have used? What will the toaster of the future look like?

7. **Questions should require evaluating, making decisions, defending observations — leaving room for personal interests and open-ended ideas.** Which environment would you prefer to live in? Why?

Developing Activity Sheets

1. Provide students with pencils and clipboards.

2. Choose exhibits that are clearly visible and ones that a small group can gather around.

3. Direct attention to the objects, not the labels.

4. Do not make all questions fact-based. Encourage thoughtful and creative answers.

5. Write questions that require observation. Questions that require drawing and descriptive writing can be very effective.

6. Move from the simple to the complex.

7. If you want harder questions, list them as "bonus" questions.

8. Vary the activities. Include such things as: counting, making lists, drawing, multiple choice, check-offs, role-playing, imagination games, make-your-own questions, etc.

9. Provide the answers somewhere.

drawn from what the student already knows and understands. Effective questioning skills make the teacher a facilitator, encouraging investigation and analysis.

Worksheets for the recording of observations and information can be excellent tools to encourage careful looking and analysis. Worksheets should use a variety of formats. Students can draw, list, count, circle, describe, compare, measure, categorize or evaluate. They can complete a sentence, arrange articles in sequential order, rate objects on a specified scale, match lists of objects, or create their own games. They can write short stories, add details to a drawing and make timelines or graphs. A tip from the Philadelphia Museum of Art states, "Not all self-guide sheets are created equally!!! Excessive length, lack of focus, or un-rewarding exercises can doom the activity."

In summary, museum education is distinguished by its focus not on the written word, but on the powerful visual language of the object. The field trip experience should take advantage of that key difference. The museum experience should provide a varied series of activities, stressing both group interaction and individual discovery. Coupled with a well-integrated set of pre-visit activities and post-visit follow-up, the field trip becomes a key ingredient in the student's total learning experience.

References

Booth, Jeannette, Gerald H. Krockover and Paula R. Woods. *Creative Museum Methods and Educational Techniques*. Springfield, IL: Charles C. Thomas, 1982.

Falk, John H. and Lynn D. Dierking. *The Museum Experience*. Washington, DC: Whalesback Books, 1992.

Grinder, Alison L. and E. Sue McCoy. *The Good Guide: A Sourcebook for Interpreters, Docents and Tour Guides*. Scottsdale, Arizona: Iron Wood Press, 1985.

Pitman-Gelles, Bonnie. *Museums, Magic and Children*. Washington, DC: Association of Science-Technology Centers, 1981.

Voris, Helen H., Maija Sedzielarz and Carolyn P. Blackmon. *Teach the Mind, Touch the Spirit*. Chicago, IL: Field Museum of Natural History, 1986.

Hands-On, Hands-Off: Strategies for Active Participation

Bay Hallowell

Associate Curator of Education, The Carnegie Museum of Art

In the museum setting students have opportunities to develop new skills — perceptual skills — that teach them how to gather information from such objects as works of art and ancient artifacts. Learning is not a passive activity. The learner must be engaged, participating in meaningful interaction with the objects around him.

In this chapter, the concept of "hands-on" is expanded to illustrate how one museum has developed a variety of imaginative activities that place the child in the heart of the experience. These teaching strategies, though designed for an art museum setting, can be effectively adapted to many kinds of museums. They demonstrate the lively and creative nature of learning in the museum and its appropriateness for all age levels.

Focused field trips with hands-on activities in museums are an ideal way for students of all ages to learn about art, the world around them, both past and present, and about themselves as well. In the art museum setting, students not only develop new perceptual skills and acquire new information, they also use what they see and learn in their own ways. Museum objects and hands-on activities must be carefully selected and designed, keeping in mind students' developmental levels, interests and school curricula.

The following ideas for hands-on experiences during focused field trips are grounded in theories of human development and their application in museum settings and in John Dewey's book, *Art as Experience*. They are also drawn from the real life experiences of museum teachers who lead educational programs at The Carnegie Museum of Art, and from a variety of articles and materials published by colleagues in other museums. Many of them can be adapted to historic homes, natural history or science museums.

The activities are divided by appropriate age groups. Certain logistical concerns apply to each. When planning hands-on activities in museums, be sure to:

- avoid days when the museum will be crowded, i.e. holidays and the field trip "season";

- select galleries that are large enough for a group to sit in for a period of time while leaving other visitors sufficient access to the collection;

- provide enough well-prepared adults to lead small groups of no more than six to eight preschool or ten elementary school children;

- be clear on what art materials or props you are allowed to use in the galleries (this usually involves permission from curators and security personnel).

Preschool and Kindergarten Children

Young children are small, and they are just getting acquainted with the big world beyond the familiarity of their own homes and schools. Most museums, however, seem very large and very alien. Hands-on activities that help preschool and kindergarten children feel safe and comfortable throughout their visit and which bring the museum down to their own physical and psychological size are recommended.

One of the very best ways to introduce preschool and kindergarten children to an art museum is by giving them postcards of objects in the museum collection before their visit. Young children can grasp postcards easily, and they like having and holding something of their own. When they arrive at the museum, they will delight in finding "their picture" and can be guided into matching all the different parts of the "real" object with their postcard, as well as comparing the colors, textures, size and mood. Collecting museum postcards for an album, or using them for sorting games at home or school, cutting them into puzzle pieces or buying duplicates to send a friend or relative are all ways of extending the museum experience.

Playing "I Spy" in a museum gallery is a good way to encourage young children to identify colors and shapes, people and places in paintings and to form imaginative identifications with works of art. "I Spy" works equally well with abstract and realistic art: In front of a large abstract painting like *Louise, Queen of Prussia* by Joan Miró, a teacher might start by saying, "I spy a long, black curving line that looks like a road for racing cars...." While looking at *The Old King* by Georges Rouault, she might say, "I spy an old king wearing a crown and holding a flower...."

"I Spy" activities like these can be extended into improvised creative movement experiences. Children can be encouraged to "paint" the lines and shapes they see in the painting by Miró in the air or to move like them. Role-playing with a few carefully chosen props such as a cardboard crown and a box to stand on will encourage four- and five-year-olds to become a king or queen for the day in front of *The Old King*. Children's books based on "I Spy" activities can be used before, during or after a field trip to introduce and reinforce the process. (See Selected Sources.)

Tactile experiences such as allowing children to touch or try on a Japanese kimono before entering the galleries encourages learning through the senses and gives them a reason for looking at Japanese woodcuts. After identifying kimonos in the woodcuts, giving children squares of colorful, patterned origami paper will motivate them to look carefully for similar colors and patterns in the art. The origami paper can then be folded into shapes found in the woodcuts or used to create collages on the floor of the gallery.

Elementary School Children

Field trips with hands-on activities for elementary school age children which are organized around imaginative themes have several advantages. When an idea captures their imaginations, children will pay attention, look closely, and become active learners. One simple idea or theme can make the diversity and number of objects in the museum less overwhelming to them. Creative movement experiences and matching games provide appropriate physical outlets for children in this age range.

— ROBERT P. RUSCHAK PHOTOGRAPHY

Young children enjoy role-playing with a few simple props.

An example of a popular theme at The Carnegie Museum of Art is dragons. Children are invited to take a trip back in time to visit the Middle Ages, then go on a dragon hunt in the Hall of Architecture where large plaster casts of cathedral facades and tombs containing a variety of fierce dragons are exhibited. The dragon hunt concludes with a visit to the Asian collection to see a friendly dragon incised on a Chinese tomb tablet — quite a contrast

with the evil, fire-breathing monsters of the Western world and an appropriate way to develop multicultural awareness. Younger students can "capture" each dragon they find by holding an imaginary camera and pretending to make it click. Elementary school students of all ages enjoy sketching their favorites using waterbase markers on paper. The sketches can be collected into books (with stories added later) or developed into paintings, clay sculptures, or papier mache puppets after the gallery visit.

Storytelling followed by sketching which is related to a specific object stimulates children to use and develop their observation skills, to identify personally with the objects, and to use their imaginations. Seated comfortably near a large bust of Athena, a museum teacher tells the story of how and why the goddess Athena turned the lovely maiden, Arachne, into a spider. As the story unfolds with references to Athena's classical features, her necklace, and her helmet, students look for these details and form pictures in their minds of Arachne's incredible transformation. This mental store of images will enhance their sketches as they draw themselves as a god or a goddess after the story is told.

Creative movement experiences related to the elements and principles of architecture in museums are both effective and enjoyable. Pairs of children can become arches and pediments. Groups of children can form columns, arcades, pyramids and domes. This physical activity and interaction is often a relief from the "please don't touch" quality of museum visits and can redirect rambunctious tendencies. Students also enjoy working with blocks in museum spaces as a way of experiencing and understanding the architecture around

— ROBERT P. RUSCHAK PHOTOGRAPHY

Drawing activities in the gallery follow an observation game and invite a creative response.

them. (Sets of small wooden blocks or foam blocks are available in most museum shops.) Concepts such as colonnades, crenellations, facades, piazzas and pinnacles become more manageable and more meaningful when they can be manipulated on a smaller-than-life scale.

Visual aids that have been prepared ahead of time help elementary students focus on the elements of realistic and abstract art and understand how color, line and shape create composition. As pre-cut cardboard shapes are held up by the teacher, students identify the same shapes in the painting *Cape Cod Afternoon* by Edward Hopper. These shapes can then be arranged like puzzle pieces by the students on the floor of the gallery to form the areas of light and shadow that make up Hopper's representation of a house at the seashore. Students will also enjoy creating their own house collages using pre-cut paper in the shape of houses in the gallery.

Contemporary artist Sol LeWitt used color and line in *Wall Drawing Number 340* to create the illusion of the

— ROBERT P. RUSCHAK PHOTOGRAPHY

Visual aids help students find design elements in a painting and encourage their awareness of shapes, lines and colors.

same color looking like two different colors. This abstraction becomes fascinating to students as they perform similar experiments with squares of brightly colored construction paper while seated in front of the painting. When abstract art is made concrete in tangible ways such as this, it becomes more accessible.

Middle and High School Students

Many middle and high school teachers find that gallery activity sheets are an effective way of making museum visits meaningful for their students. Most activity sheets encourage art criticism, directing students to analyze and interpret what they see by making specific observations and responses. Creative writing assignments, on the other hand, encourage adolescents to explore their own identities as well as to look carefully.

A starting point for creative writing in an art museum is the "Fictionary Game" in which students make up their own titles for several paintings and write them on cards. After the cards are collected and mixed up together, along with the correct title, the group guesses which title is the right one. Students earn one point for guessing the right title and one point for fooling someone. Working with five or six paintings, ranging from realistic to abstract, with a group of eight students is recommended.

Focusing on a portrait such as *Peasant* by Bastien-LePage and reading Wordsworth's poem "The Solitary Reaper" aloud will help students discover the parallels between visual and verbal forms. They can then write about a portrait of their own choosing, describing what the person depicted might be thinking, or having an imaginary dialogue with that person. A similar type of activity works well with landscapes. After close scrutiny of various landscapes and listening to related poetry read aloud, students imagine being in a particular scene in a painting, then describe their feelings about the experience in words. In a recent creative writing workshop at The Carnegie Museum of Art, the following poem was written about *Pace des Lices, St. Tropez* by Paul Signac:

The sun is shining bright.
Sometimes it gets too warm for me,
So I sit on the bench,
Underneath a couple of trees.
Here the ground is covered with flowers
And the trees stretch their limbs to the sky
Like hungry babies.

The wind blows
Cooling everything off
Including me.

I feel relaxed and calm here.
It is so beautiful,
I forget my chores.

Another gust of wind hits me.
I lie down on the bench.
All around me
Leaves and flowers dance with glee in the cool breeze.

I'm feeling sleepy now.
I'll take a little nap.
But if I sleep too long,
Wake me.
For I wish to see this day again
Before it is over.

> — by Mike Montedore
> *Age 15*

Searching for stories in paintings enables students to appreciate their dramatic qualities, then to create dramatic moments using their own words. Writing a brief diary entry for a "character" is a good warm-up exercise for writing a more extensive story based on another painting of their choice.

Focused field trips with hands-on activities make full use of the potential of museum objects to awaken students' curiosity and the process of active inquiry and learning. Working with materials in the museum setting with a specific purpose will help break the barrier of "hands-off" which can so easily cause students of all ages to lose interest. Games, sketching, creative art projects, props, and movement experiences provide a repertoire of formats from which to create a vibrant and memorable day.

References

Chetelat, Frank. "The Museum-To-Classroom Connection: A Unique Drawing Experience," *Museologist*, Winter, 1981.

Dewey, John. *Art as Experience*. New York: Capricorn, 1958.

Jensen, Nina (ed.). "Children, Teenagers and Adults in Museums," *Museum News*, May/June, 1982.

Judson, Bay. "Do You See What I See?" *School Arts*, March, 1983.

Judson, Bay. "That's Ugly!" *School Arts*, October, 1983.

Mayer, Susan M. "Alternatives to Me-You-Zeums," *Art Education*, March, 1978.

Micklethwait, Lucy. I Spy. New York: Greenwillow, 1992.

Phillips, Susan J. and William Endslow. "On a Treasure Hunt," *School Arts*, vol. 80, No. 5.

Wilson, Forrest. *What It Feels Like to Be A Building*. Washington, D.C.: The Preservation Press, National Trust for Historic Preservation, 1988.

Wolf, Aline D. *Mommy, It's a Renoir*. Altoona, PA: Parent Child Press, 1984.

School Outreach Programs and Materials

Mary D. Houts

Assistant Director and Curator of Education,
Hershey Museum

What happens when the students cannot come to you? As school budgets are increasingly constrained and field trip policies become more restrictive, a growing school audience will not have the experience of visiting the museum. Recognizing the need to make collections and the ideas they represent available to a wide school audience, many museum educators are using "outreach" programs as creative alternatives to the field trip experience.

Many real impediments exist that prevent students from coming to us, but outreach programs and materials can enliven the classroom by taking museum-related experiences directly to the school. Outreach programs and materials are also important educational tools in their own right, often providing a wider variety of experiences than can be presented in the museum setting.

Off-site programs may also augment the museum field trip, setting the scene for the visit ahead or building on a previous outing. This chapter details a variety of specific outreach programs and presents guidelines for their development.

"Outreach" — a term that encompasses a wide variety of programs developed to be used off site — is an important component of the school services of any type of museum. School outreach programs broaden the impact of a museum's educational resources by enlarging both the numbers of students reached and the ways in which they are taught. A great variety of formats exist. Some require a museum staff member or volunteer to present them; others can be used by teachers on their own. The programs can be as simple as a selection of loan objects for classroom use or as complex as a traveling theatrical production. This chapter will describe a range of possibilities.

Outreach Programs Requiring Museum Staff Presentation

Classroom Visits

Classroom visits usually consist of a museum staff member or volunteer making a presentation at a school with the help of audio-visual materials and/or artifacts. The program may also include other teaching materials such as worksheets or reproductions of primary documents. The museum teacher is the facilitator, and the program is typically designed to fit the time frame of a school period — usually forty-five minutes to an hour and a half, if periods are combined.

For older students, the programs are often in a lecture or demonstration format. For younger grades, however, the classroom visit is more likely to be designed in the form of a "hands-on" educational activity. A particularly engaging example is the Charleston (South Carolina) Museum's "Eggventures" which bring "eggciting, eggsploration eggsperiences" into primary classrooms during which students study charts and slides, examine objects from the museum's collections and do some simple experiments.

While slides are still the most commonly used visuals, some museums are now incorporating videotapes into their classroom programs. The Arizona Historical Society provides "History to Go" lessons for grades four through twelve. During these hour-long sessions, docents use a fifteen-minute video-tape along with the costumes and artifacts they bring for students to handle.

PITTSBURGH HISTORY AND LANDMARKS FOUNDATION

Two "Portable Pittsburgh" docents present a program at a Pittsburgh public school. "Clyde" is a wooden life preserver.

Demonstration/participation programs are another popular form of classroom presentation. The Jefferson County Historical Society of Watertown, New York brings "The Age of Homespun" and "Paper-mills and Papermaking" to the schools in this manner. Slides and literature on each subject are available for use by the teacher to prepare the students for the sessions. During the classroom visit, the museum educator demonstrates spinning or papermaking, and the students get a chance to try as well.

The use of primary source materials such as prints, photographs, letters and maps is also well suited for the classroom setting. The Historical Society of Pennsylvania's "History on the Go" programs for students from ages nine through fourteen include these kinds of two-dimensional materials as well as three-dimensional objects. The National Archives of the Mid-Atlantic Region has developed ten programs on such varied topics as "The Bill of Rights" and "Child Labor in the Textile Mills," which incorporate analysis and interpretation of facsimiles of the original documents. Teachers can choose either to have a classroom presentation or to have the program incorporated into their visit to the Archives building.

For those museums who can spare the staff or volunteer time, classroom visits are an excellent preparation for a museum tour. The Cumberland County (Pennsylvania) Historical Society is firmly committed to the pre-tour school visit. The Society's educator visits the classroom for a presentation with slides and artifacts before almost every tour. As part of an innovative collaborative program, the National Cathedral and the National Building Museum in Washington, D.C. send educators to present a hands-on orientation the day before a class is scheduled for its tour of both institutions.

First-person narrations can enliven history in a school setting. Here Rich Pawling, former park ranger at Hopewell Furnace National Historic Site, recreates a worker from the Furnace's past.

Assemblies

Assemblies provide an opportunity to reach a large number of students at one time with exciting, dramatic and memorable experiences. Some notable examples are the "Traveling Science Shows" presented by the Franklin Institute on such topics as "Electricity," "Flight," and "Hot and Cold," or the

theatrical productions by the Minnesota Science Museum's theater program, which are sent to schools throughout the state.

The challenge, of course, is that even one-person performances require a high level of initial investment as well as skills and talents not always available within a museum education staff. However, museums might explore collaboration as a means of developing an assembly-style production. Local secondary schools, colleges or even community theater groups may have resources to add. Joining forces with others might also encourage funding from local foundations.

Vans or Buses

A "mobile museum" is another interesting form of school outreach. The new Susquehanna Art Museum has started to function in Harrisburg, Pennsylvania with a converted bus ("Van Go!"), which houses an art exhibition and travels to area schools. There, docents give twenty-five minute tours to approximately fifteen students at a time. Similarly, Artrain, Inc. of Michigan takes a variety of changing art exhibits to communities that lack museum facilities.

Mobile museums are especially valuable for extending the museum experience beyond the typical "walls" of the institution. They do, however, require significant funding over a substantial time period in order to be cost effective.

Outreach Materials That Do Not Depend on Accompanying Staff

Audio-Visual Materials

Both as preparation for tours and for use on their own, audio-visual materials are a particularly useful means by which museums can provide classroom presentations without having to send an educator into the school.

Slide packets, accompanied by written materials, taped commentary or teachers' guides, are the most common type of audio-visual materials prepared by museum education departments. They are usually designed either to provide museum tour orientation or to present a specific classroom lesson. However, some museums, such as the Allentown Art Museum, have developed packets that can be used for either purpose.

Videotapes are an attractive alternative to slides. The Arizona Historical Society has produced a wide variety of fifteen- to sixty-minute programs available as videotapes or slide packets in both elementary and secondary school versions. The primary drawback of videotapes, however, is their cost. They are considerably more expensive to produce than slide packets. However, many museums have cut costs dramatically by teaming up with the audio-visual department of a local high school or college. Since the production of the videotape provides their students with a learning experience, the department is usually willing to undertake the project at low or no cost to the museum. Through such an arrangement, the Hershey Museum produced a videotape to provide in-school pre-visit orientation for pre-school and primary grades.

Loan Objects

Another way to bring the museum to the classroom without an educator is to provide loan objects, both reproductions and original artifacts. These are accompanied by written background materials, suggestions for classroom lessons and activities, and sometimes additional audio-visual components. There is a long history for this form of museum outreach. One of the earliest of the lending programs, and one of today's most elaborate and extensive programs, is that of the Newark Museum. It was envisioned as a three-dimensional lending library when it was established in 1912. Over 15,000 objects now make up this lending collection which includes artifacts, scale models, reproductions and costumed figures.

It is common for museums to lend groups of objects based on a subject or theme. Chester County Historical Society's "Traveling Trunks," for instance, address such themes as Lenni Lenape children, the Civil War experience in Chester County and the operation of the Underground Railroad in the county.

While loan objects can be of benefit even with a minimum of accompanying information, most museums include detailed teachers' guides. The "Loancases" of the Jefferson County (New York) Historical Society include a teachers' guide, suggestions for activities, edited documents, slide/tape sets and enlarged prints of appropriate graphics. Some of the Hershey Museum's loan kits include posters with pictures and text which can be used with the artifacts to set up learning stations in a classroom. Some include pictures with rings or mounts so the pictures can be easily pinned to bulletin boards.

The inclusion of teachers' guides and related teaching materials helps to assure constructive use by teachers, but The Franklin Institute in Philadelphia goes a step further. They give workshops for teachers in how to use their "Museum-to-Go" science activity kits. Such instruction can be incorporated into teacher in-service programs or can even be presented at teacher open-houses each year.

Like any hands-on materials used in school programs, loan objects undergo a great deal of hard use. Therefore, they must be part of a designated education collection. There is no justification for subjecting objects in a museum's permanent collections to continual handling. Even though it is understood that education collection artifacts will be subjected to hard use, they need to be treated with respect. Because there will be no museum educator to oversee their use, they will be especially vulnerable to damage.

Various methods can help you deal with this problem.

1. Include explicit instructions to the teacher on object handling.
2. Have one student activity address the need for preserving objects.

3. Protect very vulnerable objects in such packaging as plexiglass boxes which allow students to look at them closely without touching them directly.

4. Place small objects in boxes or affixed to a backing to prevent loss.

5. Select durable containers, such as trunks, suitcases, or portfolios to protect contents.

6. Divide interiors with foam or other durable materials to separate objects.

7. Label each section with the name of the object to be repacked in each particular position.

8. Affix a clear packing list on the lid of the trunk or box so that teachers can check off each item when repacking.

Heavy corrugated cardboard boxes with firmly fitting lids have been used for years for the Hershey Museum kits and have withstood considerable wear. They are not extraordinarily heavy or expensive.

How the objects will be transported is another aspect of lending that must be considered. Due to cost and possible mishap, the mails or private delivery services are usually not an option. Most museums have found the best system is to have the teacher pick up and return the materials. It is also worth checking with the delivery system of your regional school district or Intermediate Unit to see if there are options for providing direct delivery to the schools.

Curriculum Units and Individual Lesson Plans

It is generally agreed that secondary school students are a difficult audience for museums to reach. Complicated school schedules make museum visits difficult logistically, and rigidly apportioned class time make "extras" hard to fit in. Developing curriculum units and individual lesson plans in close cooperation with teachers is one way to work with this challenge.

One of the most elaborate and far-reaching examples of curriculum development is a project at the National Building Museum. Their "Design-wise" program is being developed to introduce design into traditional curricula. At the end of five years of piloting, they will have developed three different curriculum models for use by schools nationwide.

Most museum-produced curriculum materials are much more circumscribed, however. Primary source documents unobtainable elsewhere are often the basis for such curriculum units and lesson plans. The National Archives has produced a series of twelve teaching units which include reproductions of documents as well as slides and tapes. Their rich collections allow them to interpret such broad topics as "The Constitution," "The 1920s," and "The Great Depression and The New Deal." However, institutions with more narrowly based collections can still provide curriculum materials if they address a specific teaching need. Thus, the Missouri Historical Society, for instance, has produced three units on "St. Louis in American History."

Individual lesson plans can also be helpful to schools. The Hershey Museum's "Hitchhiker's Guide to the Museum" provides fifteen different lesson plans based on document reproductions, slides, and, in one case, a loan object, that can be integrated by teachers of American History into already existing school-developed curriculum units.

Getting Started — Basic Guidelines

Three guidelines are helpful when developing any type of school programming, including outreach.

1. The program should support the museum's mission statement.
2. The program should reflect the museum's collections.
3. The program should fill a felt need in the school community.

These guidelines provide focus, accountability, and, in the end, products that get used. Numbers one and two are straightforward. If the program topic cannot directly apply, there is no justification for becoming involved in the project. Guideline number three requires more work, but is crucial to the success of the outreach programming. No matter how well a program fits a museum's mission or collections, if schools are not interested, the project will sit unused on a shelf, not worth the time, money or effort invested. The Newark Museum's lending collection is directly geared to the curriculum of the Newark Public Schools. The Missouri Historical Society has correlated their classroom programs with the state-mandated Core Competencies and Key Skills.

Getting School Input

Museums must take an active role in discovering what the needs of the school community are. Curriculum directors and teachers rarely seek out museum resources.

Be fully prepared before contacting school representatives to discuss how the museum can help fill curricular needs. Use the following checklist to prepare for your contact.

- Know your museum's resources. Determine what is available from the collections and in what form — objects, slides, reproductions, documents.
- Prepare many ideas for the different forms a program might take.
- Have realistic information about the economics of developing and providing programs. Prepare a budget that includes the program's costs, sources of funding and charges for your services.
- Be prepared to maintain a flexible, cooperative attitude. If one idea won't work, perhaps another will.

■ Determine before calling what information is needed and what questions must be asked.

There are also many formats for getting teacher input. All are useful in finding out what schools can really use in outreach programming. Teachers who take part in planning also take a special interest in using and sharing the programs they help develop. The following are some formats that have been successful.

■ Form a short-term focus group.
■ Form an advisory committee of teachers/curriculum coordinators which meets on a regular basis and has an ongoing dialogue about museum-school partnership programs.
■ Hire a teacher consultant(s) or intern(s) for weekend or summer work on a project.
■ Work with teachers from a single grade level to plan a program targeted to their curricular needs.
■ Work with the curriculum coordinator from an individual school or district to develop a series of programs for each grade level.
■ Develop a needs assessment questionnaire for the teachers and curriculum coordinators at a specific grade level.

Costs and Funding

Outreach programming does not have to be extraordinarily expensive. Just as there are a wide range of outreach formats available, costs, too, can range widely.

School representatives are generally willing to give advice on programs free of charge if their time is used judiciously —usually in one or two meetings. A more professional commitment, such as honorarium, travel and expenses, should be arranged for long-term consulting. If materials are being developed by teachers, the teachers should be paid. Often school districts pay teachers for curriculum development and for in-service credits. The museum may be able to work under these headings so that funding comes directly from the schools. Additional costs include reproductions, photography, printing, packaging and staff expenses. The more in-house construction and development that can be done, the lower the financial outlay.

Outreach programs are excellent projects for which to seek outside funding. Individual donors and foundations are often attracted to the fact that, for a relatively moderate cost, the museum can reach a large number of students. The same rationale is appropriate when building outreach programming costs into the institutional budget.

Getting the Word Out

Once outreach programs are developed, they need to be publicized. Targeted mailings are the most direct way to reach schools. There are, however, many other approaches as well. These include presentations at in-service days, grade-level meetings and school-wide teacher meetings. Materials can be introduced through continuing education courses for teachers at local colleges or within such presenting organizations as the Intermediate Units. Museum educators can also get on the programs of regional and state-wide professional meetings for teachers. Contact Parent Teacher Organizations (PTOs) also, as many schools use their PTOs to provide funding for such classroom extras as outreach programs.

The museum should be willing to conduct training courses on the use of new materials, either at the schools or at the museum. Introductory sessions, such as those provided by the Franklin Institute, can be turned into mini-courses for which credit may be obtained by the participants through their individual districts or Intermediate Units.

Summary

Outreach programming for schools increases the effectiveness of museum education. It is not only an avenue for reaching students who cannot come to the museum, it also exposes students and teachers to museum teaching methodology. Outreach programming can encourage the object-based teaching methods used during museum tours and can share the insights that come directly from a face-to-face encounter with the objects and documents found only in our collections. The development of outreach programs is a premier example of the effectiveness of school and museum collaboration. It encourages the sharing of both financial and human resources to the mutual benefit of both institutions.

The Community as Classroom

Diane C. DeNardo

Director of Education and Marketing,
Pittsburgh History and Landmarks Foundation

The observational skills taught through museum education programs can extend beyond the walls of the museum. Many museum-school partnerships have viewed the community as an extended classroom, exploring such topics as architecture, community planning, geography, and environmental issues. Museums can be educational leaders in these partnerships as well, taking the concept of outreach even further than its traditional definition.

The Pittsburgh History and Landmarks Foundation is a unique museum without walls. Founded as a historic preservation organization in 1964, it identifies education as one of its primary goals. The school programs developed by the Foundation provide a series of model projects for the incorporation of the community into the curriculum. Four projects are described here as case studies. Each program includes the principles of museum education and offers sound and workable concepts to museums who may also seek to link students with the visible heritage of their surroundings.

This chapter will discuss some of the particular programs developed by The Pittsburgh History and Landmarks Foundation, a non-profit historic preservation organization serving Allegheny County in Pennsylvania. One of its most important purposes is to educate the public about the history, architecture, character and culture of the Pittsburgh region. The Foundation uses the community as its classroom. Its programs can be adapted by other institutions who view the built environment as an extension of their focus. The Foundation's experience becomes a case study for the teaching of architecture and community development.

Since its founding, education has been a primary goal of Landmarks. In 1984 Landmarks received a major grant for the purpose of creating a Revolving Fund for Education. The concept of a revolving fund is simple and has proven successful. Education programs are created that generate revenue that is returned to replenish the fund. Occasionally, additional grants are secured to fund a specific education program, and those grants also replenish the fund. Landmarks is paid to teach the courses and workshops

that it creates. It charges modest fees for public tours and lectures, sells publications and videos and rents slide shows and exhibits to schools and community groups.

Educational resources and programs for schools include slide presentations, teacher in-service courses, publications and curricula, bus and walking tours, in-school programs, lectures, workshops, a video, family programs and traveling exhibits. Four of these programs will be highlighted in this chapter: *Highs and Lows of Pittsburgh*, a walking tour; *Portable Pittsburgh*, an in-school program; *Architecture: The Building Art*, a traveling exhibit; and *Landmark Survivors*, an educational videotape.

HIGHS AND LOWS OF PITTSBURGH

Highs and Lows of Pittsburgh, a walking tour, is an example of how Landmarks uses the community as classroom. The tour was first created for families, but was so popular that is was made available as a field trip for individual classes.

The tour, as its name suggests, offers participants an opportunity to explore Pittsburgh from up "high" to down "low." A ride on the Monongahela Incline offers a chance to learn about the city from atop Mount Washington, where people can view the city from 400 feet above its river banks. The tour docent explains the layout of the city, significant buildings and bridges, various forms of transportation, and surrounding rivers and neighborhoods.

A ride on the subway takes the group under the city, where the exploration continues. The group follows an underground tunnel connecting two downtown office

PITTSBURGH HISTORY AND LANDMARKS FOUNDATION

Students on a neighborhood walking tour document the architecture of the buildings.

towers, and from there, takes a ride to the top of one of Pittsburgh's tallest skyscrapers. The lookout over the city is the perfect time to explore the architecture of the tops of buildings.

Then along the city streets, students participate in a scavenger hunt searching for gargoyles, lions, and other architectural treasures. The tour ends at a graveyard adjoining an historic landmark church. Students learn to make a tombstone rubbing —and in the process, take home a piece of Pittsburgh history.

The *Highs and Lows of Pittsburgh* tour is comprehensive. It offers an overview of Pittsburgh's history, transportation systems, architecture and both historic and recent development. Landmarks also has available a lending library of slide presentations documenting the history and architecture of Pittsburgh, and teachers are encouraged to use one of the presentations before the walking tour as an introduction to their students.

— PITTSBURGH HISTORY AND LANDMARKS FOUNDATION

"Highs and Lows of Pittsburgh" ends with students doing tombstone rubbings at Trinity graveyard in downtown Pittsburgh.

LOGISTICS

- *The Highs and Lows of Pittsburgh* is appropriate for students in grades three through eight.
- Each tour is personally arranged and teachers are specifically asked: What objectives do you have for this tour? How does this tour fit into your curriculum?
- Teachers receive a written confirmation outlining the arrangements made over the phone. In addition, the tour docent calls the teacher 2-3 days prior to the tour to re-confirm the details.

- When the docent meets the tour, she/he has a copy of the itinerary which includes the teacher's objectives.
- Groups are no larger than twelve students for a tour docent.
- Teachers are to provide a chaperone for each group of twelve.
- Classes enjoy eating lunch in one of the city's parklets, or arrangements can be made at an inexpensive eating facility.

Landmarks docents are trained to lead tours for all ages and receive special training to work with school students. They are taught how to involve students through questioning techniques and activities along the way, and they are trained to adjust their tour to meet any specific objectives a teacher may have. For example, a science class may be interested in the structure of buildings, where other groups might want to emphasize transportation systems, the urban environment, the visual art of architecture or Pittsburgh's history.

Landmarks is responsible for: determining and incorporating each group's specific objectives; providing pre-trip activities; making arrangements to enter buildings; having transportation passes for the group; providing a well-trained docent; and providing post-trip activities for follow-up instruction and discussion. The teachers are responsible for all other logistical arrangements from paying all fees to providing chaperones.

PORTABLE PITTSBURGH

This in-school program is designed for students in grades three through eight, but is frequently adapted for older students and adult audiences. *Portable Pittsburgh* docents bring a traveling kit to classrooms to unfold the history of Pittsburgh and western Pennsylvania. The kit includes artifacts, large reproductions of historic city views and maps, documents and a huge, scrolling timeline. The hour-long presentation includes a cross-section of what life was like during six eras in Pittsburgh's 200-year history, examining transportation, work, family life, architecture, local "heroes," and change in general.

Like many outreach programs, *Portable Pittsburgh* uses well-trained docents to present the classroom program. The docents receive a training manual, a ten-week course, an opportunity to observe "master docents" in action, and then teach in teams before making their first solo presentation. They are also observed by the program coordinator and are required to present at least one program per month.

Landmarks also provides teachers with a guide that includes introductory and follow-up activities and ideas for classroom projects. Teachers are encouraged to send copies of their students' work to Landmarks for publication in the membership newsletter.

ARCHITECTURE: THE BUILDING ART

Architecture: The Building Art is a traveling exhibit, funded by a grant from PPG Industries. The exhibit is an interdisciplinary resource which stays in the school for a one-month period, allowing each class to benefit from the hands-on learning. Nine display panels define the basic goals of architecture and illustrate these goals through color photographs of historic landmarks and modern structures. Teachers and students learn about building use, structure and appearance. Hands-on activity tables offer students an opportunity to design a building to meet a client's needs, to build a bridge that will not collapse, and to handle building materials such as marble, glass, steel, brick and terra cotta.

In conjunction with the exhibit, Landmarks has compiled a resource list of architects who are volunteering their time to meet with classes of elementary school students to discuss architecture and the built environment. The architects discuss their field of expertise, architecture in general, and present students with slides showing examples of their work. The architects also provide advice and feedback to the students on classroom architecture projects.

— PITTSBURGH HISTORY AND LANDMARKS-FOUNDATION

After learning about building structure, students designed a bridge that withstood the weight of a set of blocks and a set of encyclopedias.

To prepare teachers for the most effective use of the exhibit and its accompanying materials, Landmarks' director of education presents an introductory teacher workshop at the school. Ideas are presented on how the exhibit can be used with all subjects and grade levels. Teachers become acquainted with activities to do before the exhibit arrives, during its stay, and follow-up activities which could extend over the school year. Schools are also encouraged to involve parents and the community in the unit of study.

Information on the exhibit, and all of Landmarks' programs, is available in an educational brochure. The Architects-in-Schools program was introduced through a special letter to principals. As part of the program follow-up, each teacher and administrator who has participated in the project is asked to return an evaluation form.

LANDMARK SURVIVORS

This forty-minute educational video is based on an earlier traveling exhibit of the same name. The video highlights the "life stories" of seven architectural landmarks in Pittsburgh and Allegheny County: The Allegheny County Courthouse and Jail, Smithfield Street Bridge, Fort Pitt Blockhouse, Clayton (the Pittsburgh home of industrialist Henry C. Frick), Fort Pitt Boulevard, Station Square, and Kennywood Park. These landmarks provide a backdrop to discuss the importance of understanding the built environment and historic preservation. Themes presented in the program include:

— PITTSBURGH HISTORY AND LANDMARKS FOUNDATION

Stefani Ledewitz, an architect, uses a model to discuss architecture with a first grade student at Chartiers Elementary School in Pittsburgh.

- how buildings reflect the history and culture of a community;
- what constitutes a landmark;
- the reasons these particular landmarks have survived;
- the people involved in historic preservation, including community and neighborhood organizations, private citizens, historical organizations, architects, city and county planning commissions, politicians, local and state historic preservation organizations;
- the value of historic preservation.

As a collaboration between a local community organization and an area school district, the program serves as a model for other organizations. *Landmark Survivors* was a collaboration between the Pittsburgh History and Landmarks Foundation and the Fox Chapel School District. High school seniors in the "Advanced Production" television course participated in the production as part of a year-long project. Students videotaped the seven landmarks and over 100 historic photographs. They also participated in the taping of the narration and the video's editing. The work which involved students was done during regular school hours as part of school-sanctioned field trips and also voluntarily on Saturdays.

Landmark Survivors includes interviews with area engineers and historians discussing local landmark preservation projects. Through rare historic photographs and current videotape, each landmark is shown from its building date to the present day. Designed specifically for high school students, teacher in-service courses and adult education courses, this visual journey also illustrates much about the historical development of Pittsburgh.

A letter describing the video and project was sent to all high school social studies departments in Allegheny County. A description and order form was also sent to each school library in the county. A copy of the video is available to teachers, on loan, through the Allegheny Intermediate Unit's Film Distribution Library. Each video is accompanied by a six-page teachers' guide offering background information, suggestions for introduction and follow-up activities, and a description of the video content.

The four programs detailed here are just a small sampling of the educational resources available through the Pittsburgh History and Landmarks Foundation. By concentrating on the development of a variety of formats for outreach, Landmarks has reached thousands of students. Each program succeeds through the formula of a well-developed and focused program, effective pre-visit and post-visit activities, close communication with teachers, and a clear sense of teaching objectives.

Image Watching:
A Case Study
in Critical Thinking

Robert W. Ott, Ph.D.

Professor of Art Education,
The Pennsylvania State University, University Park

*How do you teach a child to think — to ask questions, make obser-
vations and form judgments? Every educator is ultimately concerned with the stimulation of these "higher-order" critical thinking
skills. It is not enough to elicit rote memorization or superficial
knowledge. The true goal of education is to prepare students as critical thinkers with the skills to ask significant questions, gather and
analyze data, study and evaluate new experiences, and integrate
knowledge and understanding throughout their lives.*

*The museum setting provides a unique environment for the teach-
ing of critical thinking skills. Previous chapters have considered the
application of learning theories, the role of focused activities and
the need for active participation in museums. The following case
study examines a systemic teaching process called* Image Watching,
*a step-by-step approach to the development of critical thinking skills
in a museum environment.*

Image Watching *has been developed as a strategy for learning about
art, but its systematic approach can also be adapted to the study of
many disciplines. The editor includes a sample program presented in
a history museum at the conclusion of this chapter. Museum collections, whether art, craft or historic artifact are touchstones for intellectual thought. Learning from any of these collections requires the
same emphasis on observation, inquiry and analysis as a prelude to
understanding.*

Museums offer a provocative source for a student's intellectual development — a source best used when educators effectively plan for the teaching
of higher-order and critical thinking skills. At the core of this teaching is an
individualized and sequential *process* built on the museum's primary source
material. This chapter will detail the use of a highly successful process known
as *Image Watching*.

Objects are literally the textbooks of museums, but learning to read these "textbooks" requires a systematic intellectual approach with emphasis on the skills of comprehension, conceptualizing, problem solving and higher-order content synthesis. Critical thinking processes are systems which contain steps, stages or phases which enable learners to reach higher-level thinking skills while working with museum objects. The systemic teaching process known as *Image Watching* combines the development of thinking skills with the creative process of an artistic production or performance. It has been successfully used over the past decade throughout Pennsylvania and other states, as well as in Canada, Holland, Germany and Brazil.

The *Image Watching* system has five teaching categories. These categories are sequential and are known as 1) describing, 2) analyzing, 3) interpreting, 4) funding, and 5) disclosing. Each builds upon the other, evolving into a perceptual, conceptual and interpretive critical thinking process for comprehending the meaning of objects in the museum (Ott, 1989).

Critical Thinking Categories

The teaching process begins with the *describing* stage. The initial encounter with the object is focused on visual perception and observation. A teacher needs to provide sufficient time for this process to evolve and, in fact, needs to assist students in learning how to see objects. The role of perception is not taken lightly; it is essential to the entire process. In the describing category, students make an inventory, listing all of the details they can see in the object under critical study.

Questions designed by the teacher reinforce this inventory. Students might be asked to observe by categories: first list the objects in a painting, then the colors and shapes. They might be asked to focus on elements, e.g., to describe lines and repeat those lines in a drawing. Each question will be designed to draw the student deeper into the process of seeing. What is actually seen on the surface of the object needs to be elicited and noted by the student before further thinking processes occur. In preparing such a list, students gain confidence derived from looking carefully, noting details and confirming their personal perceptions.

When teachers organize the activities into a formal learning packet, a page might include graphic images which evoke students' perceptions. Some teachers use the "part of a whole" concept, providing details of objects or fragments for students to consider closely. The list generated in this stage provides the data for critical thinking. It is raw data, perceived and untreated at this point, and will provide the basis for further inquiry.

Analytical Skills and Criticism

Analyzing a museum object is a stimulating intellectual experience when students have acquired all of the necessary data during the describing stage. Describing is the most factual and objective step. Analyzing begins the process of inquiry and leads to questions about how and why the artwork or artifact was composed, designed, invented, or established.

Analyzing includes comparing and contrasting. The formal elements of design and composition may be the starting point for this stage. Comparing areas of color intensity, texture, detail, use of line and shape will provoke questions which search for suppositions about the object. The artist's use of high color contrasts and intensity, for example, might raise questions about the emotional content of the painting. Further inquiry may be concerned with why the artist, craftsman or creator of the object chose to express the ideas she did or how the ideas in the work under study relate to issues in society, the community or in the student's world. Often the discovery of these ideas, which give meaning to the object, precede the discovery of the artist's technique.

The materials used by the artist or craftsman to express ideas as well as the manner in which the object is executed is also of particular interest. Teachers may design worksheets requesting students to write about their understandings of the sensory qualities of color, shape and movement or the tactile qualities of specific media. As the student begins to discover the ideas and content of the object from inquiry and analysis, she will be quickly engaged in the third stage of *Image Watching*, that of interpretation.

Critical Interpretation as Learning

Often considered one of the most creative of the critical thinking skills, *interpreting* is a stage during which students discover new motivations for their interest and for learning. It is also the stage in which the teacher realizes how effective the teaching plans have been, for it is during this stage that no one answer may be correct. A student's opinions and premises are paramount. Some teachers may find they are not as open to managing the numerous ideas that often flow from students during interpretation as they might be. Others are elated by the diverse and numerous expressions of ideas and concepts that often spill forth at this stage.

Such responses, expressions and interpretive statements about art objects are a clear indication that critical thinking is evolving in students. Interpretations may be right or wrong, fully developed or undeveloped at this point, but interpreting is a higher order of thinking for every student involved in a critical thinking process. During the interpretation stage, the student places the work into a relationship or comparison with other knowledge,

objects or environments he or she has known. This stage also encourages students to express their emotional and subjective responses to the work.

At this stage a student might be encouraged to "enter" a painting, to consider what its subject might be thinking, to conjecture about what will happen next or why the artist included certain details or omitted others. The act of judgment, woven throughout *Image Watching*, is most pronounced at this stage. Unlike most criticism theories, however, *Image Watching* does not end in judgment. Further, the act of judgment is constantly held in check until students have enough insights to develop a more fully evolved and considered evaluation. By slowing down the reaction time of students and providing clear guidelines for observation and analysis, *Image Watching* encourages interpretations and judgments that are more considered and meaningful.

Nothing can be more frustrating to a student confronting new information or images than to place interpretation at the beginning of the critical thinking process. To ask first how a painting makes a student feel is a folly. Perceptions and thoughts developed through analysis need to be evolved first. Students involved in the initial processes of seeing and understanding will become more confident and secure with their judgments.

Knowledge Funds Critical Thinking

Funding adds an extension to interpretation and supports the creative production stage of *Image Watching*. In this area the student's act of interpreting museum objects is "funded" with additional knowledge made available from historical and social contexts. Sources such as critics, curators, historians, artists and craftsmen are consulted to provide students with a depth of information to add to their emerging critical thinking skills. The teacher both presents new information and encourages student research.

Students as researchers are a vital part of the evolving critical thinking process embraced by *Image Watching*. Students seek out primary sources, such as student-conducted interviews with artists, review of historical documents, study of prominent critics and reading in the extensive libraries of the school, museum or community.

The additional information acquired through funding is expected to extend the student's understanding of the object but not to supplant what he has already learned through his own processes of describing, analyzing and interpreting. Information about objects is best when it adds to the student's personal account of knowledge rather than replaces his critical thinking. Such information too often becomes the "accepted view" when presented too early in the critical thinking process.

In some funding episodes, the artist serves as the primary resource. In these cases, artists or craftsmen are actively engaged at the funding stage, but have been standing aside as observers during the early stages. Artists who experience the critical thinking of students during the first stages of *Image Watching* are often astounded at the depth of understanding and sensitivity revealed by the students. The students, in turn, hold the artist's opinions and remarks in high regard when the artist enters as a primary source in the funding stage.

Teachers designing learning portfolios should include bibliographies of reference material easily accessible to students. Teachers should encourage students to bring additional resources into this process, however, remaining flexible to student discoveries and innovative thinking. Such sources as exhibition catalogues and academic publications will give students a realization and respect for the role of scholarship in museums.

Disclosing as Higher-Level Learning

Disclosing permits students to incorporate their knowledge about a museum object through an individual act of production. Disclosing, as the final stage in *Image Watching*, is the essential difference between this and other systems of critical thinking. Disclosure is a studio activity in which the student gives tangible and public expression to his understanding of the object. "Whenever students engage in studio activities, they give physical form to a previously invisible thought. In doing so, the students disclose information to those around them." (Clark, 1991)

Disclosure may be in the form of another artwork, literary work, critical essay, poetry or any form of creative expression that incorporates the discoveries of the critical thinking process. In all cases, this production permits self-assessment through a highly articulated form of artistic activity, incorporating a realization of both process and idea.

Much of what has formerly been considered effective critical thinking has focused only upon the act of making an intelligent judgment. *Image Watching* goes a significant step further, incorporating the act of making use of intelligent judgment. The art form used by the student in the disclosing stage offers a transformation. A new work is created, inspired by a high level of understanding acquired in the museum and realized by the student's perceptions, research efforts and comprehensions. The process has thus promoted critical thinking skills to an even higher level of achievement.

The *Image Watching* process can provide a model for use by both teachers and museum educators. The steps of describing, analyzing, interpreting, funding and disclosing can be assembled into a teaching portfolio, a series of defined worksheets and activities that guide the student through activities in each stage of learning. The final stages of funding and disclosing may be achieved in the museum through a library/studio component, or they may comprise the post-visit activities. The effectiveness of the total process, however, will require a close partnership between school and museum.

A portfolio learning packet, designed by Pennsylvania teachers, enables teenagers to develop critical thinking skills during a museum visit.

The portfolio approach, developed from the teacher's or museum educator's plan, has the added advantage of becoming the student's learning record. This record of the development of critical thinking skills is captured eventually in the student-produced work, but it is also indelibly etched into the nature and character of the student and becomes a means for life-long learning.

Editor's note

Image Watching was designed for use in art museums. Its five stages — describing, analyzing, interpreting, funding and disclosing — can also be adapted to other kinds of museum settings. The following describes a program developed at Chester County Historical Society that uses a similar process in considering historic artifacts.

A group of students begin sitting in a semicircle. A contemporary iron is passed from student to student. Each makes an observation about the iron — noting materials, shapes, colors, writing, movable parts, assembly — an aspect which can be visually or tactually perceived. The museum teacher encourages observations when students get "stuck" — asking them to turn the iron over, look for specific kinds of detail, read patent numbers, touch different surfaces.

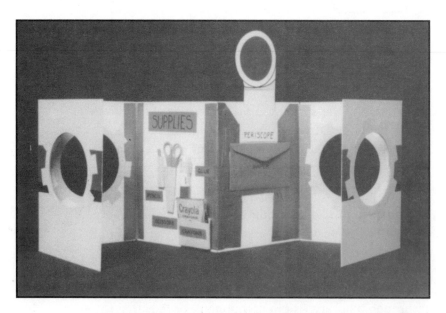

The creative production of new knowledge through the arts is encouraged by these teacher-designed portfolios for middle school students.

When the students have run out of observations, a second iron is passed around — this one a sad iron, dating to around 1800. The process is repeated. Then the students begin to analyze the differences between the two irons, noting such things as size, weight, technology, design, materials, colors, writing, and use.

Interpreting is based on the data gathered through observation and analysis. Students conjecture about what each observed detail and contrast means in terms of the lifestyles of the persons who once used or continue to use the objects. The perceptions at this point are often quite remarkable. Students have commented about such things as the writing on the iron suggesting use within a literate society and the lists of fabrics (polyesters, nylons, rayons, etc.) suggesting the role of petroleum-based products in contemporary society. Students are often asked what improvements were necessary to move from the sad iron to the modern iron and put in sequence such concepts as adding a wooden handle that would not conduct heat and providing a hollowed base into which hot coals could be placed.

Teacher-drawn cartoons reach younger students as they encourage higher-order thinking skills in museum encounters.

The funding step is supplied by a variety of sources — from a narrated set of slides about the technology of early America to reading lists for further study. The museum educator and classroom teachers have collaborated on ways in which study continues in the classroom following this exercise, often applying the same process of analysis to other kinds of objects.

Disclosing is not completed in the gallery but is suggested as a classroom post-trip activity. Students are asked to take the "past" and "present" experience into its next stage and design the iron of the "future." One school has followed this activity with an inventions fair, which has students consider not

only new ideas but new materials, technologies and designs. Other schools have built on the object analysis by having students do creative writing about living in the past with the technologies they have identified or becoming a time traveler who notes other differences across the centuries.

The activity takes the four analytical stages and adds a creative component that encourages students to apply and extend their discoveries into new areas, not only possessing new information but transforming it into personal terms.

References

Chapman, L.H. *Approaches to Art in Education*. New York: Harcourt Brace Javanovich, 1978.

Clark, Roger Allen. "Art as an Emergent School Subject," *Studies in Art Education*. Reston: National Art Education Association, 1991.

Feldman, E.B. *Becoming Human Through Art*. Englewood Cliffs, NJ: Prentice Hall, Inc., 1970.

Gardner, Howard. *The Unschooled Mind: How Children Learn and How Schools Should Teach*. Basic Books: Harper Collins, 1991.

Greene, M. *The Dialectic Freedom*. New York: Teachers College, Columbia University, 1988.

Mittler, G. *Art in Focus*. Peoria, IL: Glencoe Publishing Co., 1986.

McEvilley, T. "On the manner of addressing clouds," *Art Forum XXII*, pp. 61-71, 1984.

Ott, Robert W. "Teaching Criticism in Museums," *Museum Education: History, Theory and Practice*. Reston: National Art Education Association, 172-193, 1989.

Parsons, M.J. *How We Understand Art*. Cambridge: Harvard University Press, 1987.

Pepper, S.C. *The Basis of Criticism in the Arts*. Cambridge: Harvard University Press, 1946.

Wolf, Dennie Palmer and Nancy Pistone. *Rethinking Assessment Through the Arts*. New York: College Entrance Examination Board, 1991.

Cultural Diversity:
The Museum as Resource

Susan K. Donley

Education Specialist, WQED, Pittsburgh,
and Museum Education Consultant

*Museums for a New Century (AAM, 1984) cites society's evolving
sense of its own pluralism as a major force of change in how museums will define their mission in the years ahead. The diversity of
cultural and ethnic heritages in this country has been recognized as
a distinctive element in the American character. Americans can
build upon this diversity as a strength, or they can be weakened by
its fragmentation. Education is key to how multiculturalism can be
accepted into the national consciousness as a positive force.*

*The museum-school partnership presents a unique opportunity to
examine cultural diversity. Museum collections and exhibitions
reflect a variety of ethnic heritages and suggest new ways to integrate multicultural topics into many school disciplines. The following chapter looks closely at the leadership museums and schools
can bring to this critical topic.*

The "melting pot" — that vision in which "foreigners" eagerly flock to
American shores and willingly assimilate into one superior "American" culture
— is dead. It probably only truly existed in the wishful thinking of early twentieth-century reformers trying to make sense of the greatest wave of human
migration in history. The melting pot analogy assumed that for a society to
function peacefully and effectively, cultural differences must be eliminated.
In fact, however, social scientists have pointed out that the melting pot was
never an apt description of the United States. Many groups have not assimilat-
ed, either by their own choice or because of prejudice against them.

Census projections show that the United States is becoming more, rather
than less, culturally diverse. The term "mosaic" is now used to describe this
state of affairs and to symbolize the ideal of unity in diversity, in contrast to
the "melting pot" ideal of cultural assimilation. In the American "mosaic" (the
terms "tapestry" and "salad bowl" are also used), the nation's culture derives

its beauty and strength from many distinct cultures maintaining their own identities as they come together with a common purpose.

Educational institutions — schools, museums, and libraries alike — have struggled with the best way to restructure curriculum and programs to reflect society and prepare students to live in a "multicultural" world. While they may not know exactly what *does* work, after years of trying, they do know something about what does *not*. Museums and schools can learn from each other as they work on a solution.

What doesn't work

Schools have tended to isolate ethnic studies in pockets of the curriculum. Social studies cover a handful of ethnic heroes in text side-bars or during special "emphasis" months. Singling out ethnic-groups-of-the-month necessarily runs out of months before it runs out of groups, alienating those who have not been included! World cultures, a staple in the secondary school curriculum, has used a similar approach for decades without accomplishing the goals of multicultural education.

Mentioning famous ethnic heroes in textbook side-bars without a multicultural approach to the rest of the course material gives the impression that some people are ethnic and others are not. Another form ethnic studies takes, particularly at the elementary level, is the study of foods, crafts and holiday traditions from other lands.

These common approaches share several weaknesses. First, they focus on the unusual or extraordinary — the famous person or the quaint custom. Yet *ethnicity is commonplace*. It pervades every level of our culture from our families and communities to our nation and world. Our cultural ties help to determine everything from our language, our food, and our relationships to our emotional and political reactions. Even people who feel they have no ethnic heritage belong to an Anglo-American heritage modified by earlier native and immigrant groups (Donley, 1988).

What may work

While there may be no magic formula for what works in multicultural education, there are a few promising strategies.

Recognize the hierarchy of cultural attitudes.

Educational research has shown that people follow a definite process in developing their attitudes toward cultural diversity. Most people stop their cultural development somewhere along the way, often with disturbing results. The failure of the previous multicultural education methods can be partly explained by identifying which levels of the hierarchy they address and which they ignore. The hierarchy of developing cultural attitudes is:

1. awareness;
2. understanding/knowledge;
3. tolerance/acceptance;
4. appreciation.

Helping students advance at least to tolerance/acceptance of people from other cultures should be our minimum goal as educators. Yet most multicultural curricula — including museum exhibits and publications — focus on relaying *information* about other cultures, an approach that brings students only to the second level, that of understanding and knowledge. One of the failings of our educational system has been to assume that knowledge of other cultures alone will automatically change attitudes. In fact, understanding/knowledge can be one of the most dangerous places to stop along this hierarchy. For example, Nazi propagandists used "facts" about ethnic and political groups to reinforce stereotypes and elicit tacit public support for their systematic persecution.

To advance along the hierarchy to tolerance, acceptance, and finally, appreciation, students must be challenged beyond the acquiring of simple knowledge to the changing of previous attitudes. To effect such changes, we must prepare students with the critical thinking skills necessary to form judgments. They need to reach their own conclusions about other cultures rather than simply trusting what others — even well-meaning educators —tell them.

Teach methods as well as content.

Rather than spoon-feeding easy answers, schools and museums can help foster higher-level thinking skills by encouraging students to ask thoughtful questions. Simply learning facts stalls students at the understanding/knowledge level of the hierarchy. They must learn to reach their own conclusions, withholding judgment until all evidence is gathered and then critically analyzing each resource. This critical thinking process teaches students the most effective prejudice-reducing skill applicable to our diverse society. Museums can provide sources for analysis and can model sound, intellectual practices.

Build self-esteem.

The most important preparation students can receive for living in a multicultural society has little to do with learning about cultures! Anything that educational institutions can do to improve the self-esteem of individuals will help them —and our society as a whole — move up the hierarchy. Students need to accept and appreciate themselves and their own culture before they can risk accepting or appreciating someone from another culture. A secure person has little need to put down another person to make himself feel superior. Self-esteem is necessary for students to risk coming to their own conclusions.

Examine the role of culture in family, community, nation, world.

Multicultural education is more successful if it begins with the self and the family. Studying the culture of their own family builds students' self-esteem and gives them a basis for cross-cultural comparisons. With a basic knowledge of their own culture, they can move out in ever-growing circles to collect and analyze information about the diverse cultures interacting in their communities, in the nation and on the global level.

Integrate multiculturalism into all discipline areas.

Approaches that seamlessly integrate a multicultural perspective into educational programs all year long and in every discipline have been more successful in effecting real change than those that have segregated ethnic studies into curriculum ghettos. A powerful message is sent to students when cultural diversity is acknowledged and valued in language arts, math, science, technology, and the arts, as well as in social studies and history.

Barbara Weir, assistant archivist at Chester County Archives and Record Services, leads students through the first steps in tracing family history. Knowledge of their own cultural heritage enables students to begin the process of understanding others.

What does this mean for museums?

The potential for museums to take the lead in interpreting our culturally diverse heritage is great. After all, objects offer a natural way to cut across language and time barriers to help people understand cultures different from their own. First, however, museums must find ways to overcome several challenges built into their infrastructure.

Like schools, museums have fallen into the disciplinary ghetto trap. Traditionally, art and history museums deal with the art and artifacts of

European cultural groups, but natural history museums present the art and artifacts of non-European groups — the implication is insulting. At least the anthropologists designing modern natural history cultural exhibits recognize the importance of context in interpreting material from other cultures. When art museums have exhibited non-Western art, they have been criticized for exhibiting objects out of context. This practice unfairly subjects artifacts to the same art-for-art's-sake aesthetic as Western fine arts, a practice which leads to no understanding of the cultures of origin (Karp, Lavine, 1991).

Ellen Dissanayake points out in her essay, "Art for Life's Sake," that much of the world's creative work is not art for art's sake, so the classical rules of criticism and art history cannot be applied: "To claim that one can appreciate works from alien cultures is an imperialistic act of appropriation — molding them to one's own standards while blatantly dismissing or ignoring the standards of their makers and users." (Dissanayake, 1991, p.18)

Strategies for change

Ivan Karp and Stephen Lavine suggest in the introduction of *Exhibiting Cultures* that to be effective agents of multicultural education, museums must abandon the image of museum as temple and adopt the notion of a museum as forum (Karp, Lavine, 1991). Art museums in particular must modify their belief in a canon of great "fine art," a belief that holds true only for art in the European tradition. Ellen Dissanayake offers an alternative definition of art that lays common ground for looking at art from other cultures: "...Art, as making the things one cares about special, shaping and elaborating the ordinary to make it more than ordinary, is fundamental to everyone...." (Dissanayake, 1991, p.25)

Museums can provide a great service to school educators by pioneering new ways of looking at these works that cross our rigid art, history and natural history disciplinary lines. "Taking a Closer Look," a set of worksheets found at the end of this chapter, provides a systematic method of inquiry especially useful for looking at art from non-Western traditions. *(Editor's note: note how it parallels* Image Watching, *the critical thinking strategy defined by Dr. Robert W. Ott in the previous chapter.)*

To be forums rather than temples, museums must go beyond merely exhibiting and providing information about objects. Below are a few strategies for provoking critical thinking about cultural diversity within the museum setting.

To interpret cultural diversity, start with similarities.

In trying to cultivate tolerance, acceptance, and finally appreciation of cultural diversity, museums and schools should keep in mind a basic, but paradoxical, multicultural concept: All people share the same basic needs and values, but differ in how they meet those needs and express those values.

For example, the Smithsonian *Generations* exhibit showed how two cultures passed on the value of independence to their children in very different ways. Contemporary families in the United States allow their infants to sleep in their own rooms and cry in their cribs once they have been fed, changed and paid some attention. Bolivian Indians might find this practice barbaric — their infants sleep with their mothers and are tied to their backs throughout daily farm and household chores until they are able to keep up on foot. Then they accompany their parents everywhere to learn the skills they will need as adults. At about thirteen years of age, these children have learned everything they will need to know to survive as adults in their culture — they are independent despite being in almost constant contact with their parents.

Museums can help visitors get beyond classifying unfamiliar customs or objects as quaint or odd by interpreting the basic needs and values that motivate these customs. A teacher taking a multicultural workshop brought in a newspaper photo of a Thai woman with a gold collar permanently wrapped around her neck, elongating it. I asked the class why they thought the woman wore the neck piece. They answered, "She thinks it's attractive." "Well, what do we do to look attractive?" Before long, they were laughing that they poked holes in their ears, rolled heated rods in their hair, stood all day in shoes with heels elevated in a way that cramped their toes into a point, scraped their faces with sharp blades every morning and tied narrow fabric bands tightly around their necks. Reading "Body Rituals of the Nacirema" or David Macauley's illustrated book *Motel of the Mysteries* is a hilarious way of discovering how our material culture might be interpreted if another culture jumped to as many conclusions about us as we tend to when we try to analyze other cultures carelessly.

The Indianapolis Children's Museum organized their successful *Passport to the World* exhibit around the basic characterisitics common to all people. Within the common themes, "All people...create, celebrate, imagine, work and communicate," this major ethnographic reinterpretation explored the wonderfully diverse ways people fulfill their needs and express their values through these activities.

Make cross-cultural connections and comparisons.

Cross-cultural comparison is one very effective multicultural education strategy that lends itself well to museums. It capitalizes on the similarities/differences theme, inviting visitors to make connections to their own experiences while examining the diverse responses of human beings to their environments. Further, by teaching methods of looking at cultures, not just gathering information about them, museums can provide viewers with classification systems to use whenever they encounter a new culture.

Cross-cultural comparisons can be developed around many kinds of themes: comparisons of objects — toys, figures, clothing, tools; comparisons of the functions of artifacts — their use in celebrations, rites of passage, storytelling, daily chores; comparisons of the formal elements of art — use of pattern, color, shape, composition. The possibilities are nearly endless.

When preparing cross-cultural comparisons, avoid oversimplifying. For example, Hopi kachina masks are sacred religious objects that would be accurately compared with priests' vestments. They should not be compared with Halloween masks or dramatic masks.

Provide as much context as possible.

By definition, museums deprive objects of their contexts by bringing them to a central repository for interpretation to the public. We do not apologize for our missions, but we do need to be conscious of how our actions prohibit a truthful interpretation of objects from other cultures. For example, in the 1940s and 1950s the contemporary art world was "discovering" African art and exhibiting it in American art galleries as beautiful examples of abstraction. Such exhibits teach us more about our own aesthetic than about the cultures that produced the objects. An Ashanti fertility figure might be evaluated and appreciated by Western artists for its elegant simplification of form, but in the context of its own culture, the doll would be evaluated by whether the girl who tucked it into the back of her skirt produced a large family when she grew up.

History and natural history museums have long made use of dioramas, reenactments or period settings to provide context. Such media as photography, audio and video tapes supplement these traditional exhibit forms, and interactive media show promise as context-builders in the near future.

However, people — the makers and users of culturally significant objects — are the most important element of context. Exhibits, publications, and other museum programs can showcase makers and users of artifacts in person, on tape or in print, and interviews can be an integral part of exhibits. "Ask the Artist," a worksheet included in the appendix, outlines a simple interview viewers can conduct at a demonstration to elicit valuable contextual information.

Balance ecological (contextual) and systematic (cross-cultural) exhibits.

Cross-cultural comparisons obviously cannot be ecological and contextual. Neither can dioramas and period settings provide a systematic view of similar objects across cultures. Museums can strive to balance both styles of interpretation and stay clear about the advantages and disadvantages of each approach.

Involve people from the cultures in exhibit and program design.

To shun the "imperialism" Dissanayake disdains, museums are being urged to invite the viewpoints of the people whose culture they are trying to interpret. A recurring theme in *Exhibiting Cultures* is to "give populations a chance

to exert control over the way they are presented in museums." (Karp, Lavine, 1991, p.6) Their active involvement in the curatorial process will help insure the multiple perspectives implied by a forum, rather than a temple.

Be on the alert for stereotyping.

Museums, like schools, must resist the urge to stereotype by lumping cultures into giant categories: Africans, Native Americans, Asians. These are more accurately referred to as geo-political groups. The whole idea of multi-culturalism is that no culture is monolithic. Interpret the diversity of your own community. Encourage visitors to make cross-cultural comparisons *within* other large geo-political groups, not just between them.

Inadvertent stereotyping also occurs when information about a past cultural group is presented without updating it. Native Americans are routinely depicted in Pennsylvania museums as if they are an extinct people. On the contrary, some Native Americans still live in the state, and others whose ancestors lived here have established homes elsewhere in the nation. None of them still make a living hunting with hand-hewn stone weapons.

Help visitors see cultural diversity all around them.

Finally, remember what cultural diversity is all about and resist the urge to refer to "American" culture or "our own" culture. Our communities, our state and our nation are themselves multicultural places. We would be hard pressed to define exactly what "American culture" really is — that is, what values, lifestyles and traditions every American shares. That is both the beauty and the challenge of living in a multicultural world!

TAKING A CLOSER LOOK

**CHOOSE A WORK OF ART to look at closely.
Look at it quietly for 60 seconds. Then...**

DESCRIBE

WITHOUT LOOKING back, list what you saw:

Look again. Correct your list. What else do you see now that you missed the first time?

Sketch a miniature drawing of this art object:

What materials did the artist use? What tools did s/he use?

How many different colors can you see? What names would you give the colors?

How many different kinds of lines can you find? What words would you use to describe them?

How would you describe the object's texture? How many different textures can you find?

How would you describe its overall shape? How many different shapes exist within the overall shape?

ANALYZE

THIS WORK OF ART is mostly (check one):
- ❏ Three-dimensional
- ❏ Flat

On your sketch, mark where the focus of attention is in this art object. How has the artist drawn your eye to this spot?

Why is this spot important?

Which of the design elements are most important in this work of art—line, shape, texture, or color? Why?

How is the surface of this object decorated?

What tools and materials were used to create the decoration?

What visual elements were used to create the decoration?

Where—if at all—does the artist use pattern on the object?

Draw the repeating part of the pattern in the space below:

WHAT IMAGES—if any—does the object represent?

What is the purpose of this work of art?

Imagine (then research) the place this object was made or used. What people are around? What are they doing?

INTERPRET

What kind of architecture and plants are around?

Imagine (then research) the occasion this object was used:

What kind of day is it?

What is the weather like?

What would would you hear or smells would you smell if your were on the scene?

Imagine (then research) what the person who made this object was like:

Imagine (then research) who the owner of the object might have been:

Were they one and the same? If not, how do you think the owner acquired the object?

If you were a reporter interviewing the artist, what questions would you ask?

Research the craft and the culture it came from. Write your researched answers under your imagined answers. How close was your imagination to the truth?

EVALUATE
SPECULATE

HOW DO YOU THINK the artist felt about this object?

How do you think the user of the object felt about it?

Why do you think the artist created this work?

How are the artist's or owner's personal beliefs or values revealed?

What object in your culture serves a similar purpose? Why?

What object in your culture has a similar appearance? How?

What other art medium could this object be translated into? Why would this be a good choice?

How easy is this work of art to understand?
What else would you like to know?

Is this a work of art you would like to own?
Why or why not?

If you would not like to own this art work, why do you think it is in this collection?

References

Banks, James A. *Teaching Strategies for Ethnic Studies*, 4th Edition. Boston: Allyn and Bacon, Inc., 1987.

Berk, Ellyn. *A Framework for Multicultural Arts Education*. New York: National Arts Education Research Center, New York University, School of Education, Health, Nursing and Arts Professions.

Dissanayake, Ellen. "Art for Life's Sake." *What is Art For? Keynote Addresses, 1991 NAEA Convention*. Reston, VA; National Art Education Association, 1991.

Donley, Susan K. *A Sampler of Ethnic Crafts*. Pittsburgh, Pennsylvania Ethnic Heritage Studies Center, University of Pittsburgh, 1990.

Donley, Susan K. *Toward a Better Balance (Volumes I and II)*. Pittsburgh: Pennsylvania Ethnic Heritage Studies Center, University of Pittsburgh, 1988.

Karp. Ivan and Lavine, Stephen K., ed. *Exhibiting Cultures: The Poetics and Politics of Museum Display*. Washington, DC: Smithsonian Institution Press, 1991.

Macaulay, David. *Motel of the Mysteries*. Boston: Houghton, Mifflin, 1979.

Miner, Horace. "Body Ritual of the Nacerima." *The American Anthropologist*, vol. 58 (1956), pp. 503-507.

Suina, Joseph H. "Museum Multicultural Education for Young Learners." *Journal of Museum Education*. Volume 15, Number 1. Winter 1990.

Young, Bernard, ed. *Art Culture and Ethnicity*. Reston, VA: National Art Education Association, 1990.

Super Stuff:
An Appendix of Successful
Program Materials

Many museums across Pennsylvania have produced excellent materials to support their educational programs. Some of these fine materials have been assembled here to serve as an appendix of ideas. Included are a variety of formats for educational brochures as well as reservation, confirmation, and evaluation forms. Several kinds of pre-trip materials illustrate different approaches to preparing students for their museum visit, and post-trip assignments share useful concepts for classroom follow-up. Self-guiding materials and object-based worksheets are also included to stimulate new ideas for approaching your own collections.

The materials included, whether professionally designed or produced in-house, are indicative of the creative ideas that abound in museums large and small. This group is just a beginning. You should develop your own collection of interesting materials by requesting samples from other museums. Peruse the display tables at professional meetings and attend sessions that offer a roundtable of ideas. By sharing with one another, educators develop an ever-widening circle of ideas.

Arts-in Education Partners

Southern Alleghenies Museum of Art

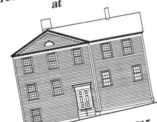

TOURS AND ACTIVITIES FOR SCHOOL GROUPS 1991-92

Educational Services

The University Museum of Archaeology/ Anthropology

Attic black figure amphorae
Neg. 2751

Game board
Neg. 79939

The University Museum
33rd and Spruce Streets, Philadelphia, PA 19104
215-898-4015/4025
Tuesday through Saturday:10:00 am to 4:30 pm
Sunday: 1:00 to 5:00 pm

THREE HOUSES:
How Erie Changed in the 19th Century
A Three-Part School Program at

The Dickson Tavern - 1815

The Cashier's House - 1839

The Watson-Curtze Mansion - 1891

HERSHEY MUSEUM

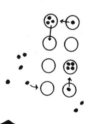

SCHOOL SERVICES
K – 12

"Ludwig Miller teacher. at the old lutheran Schoolhouse. in the year 1805." by Lewis Miller (1796-1882) of York. From the collection of the Historical Society of York County.

HISTORICAL SOCIETY OF YORK COUNTY
250 East Market Street, York, Pennsylvania 17403 ● 848-1587

EDUCATIONAL PROGRAMS
at Brandywine Battlefield

Educational Programs at Brandywine Battlefield

❖ What can be learned from an historic artifact?

❖ Why is it important to preserve old structures and historic landscapes?

❖ What do we know about the Revolutionary War soldier and his contribution to our freedom?

❖ Why are George Washington and Lafayette honored as heroes?

These questions and others will be answered during enjoyable programs designed to enable students to develop new abilities and historic perspectives. Guides in period clothing lead students through a series of discovery-oriented activities in the Education Room at Washington's Headquarters and at Lafayette's Quarters. Rules of good museum behavior and methods of learning in an historic environment will be introduced.

Tours

Tours include: a slide show, a hands-on lesson in the Education Room, a house tour (for second-graders and older), and a grade-oriented activity.

Starting times: 9:30 a.m., 10 a.m., 12:30, 1 p.m., 3 p.m.

Time required: 2–3 hours

Fee: $3.00 per student*

 * Minimum group of 12 or minimum fee of $36.00.
 * Special tours lasting more than 3 hours with additional programs will increase fee per student.

Upon Arrival at the Visitor Center

Group leaders please report to Reception Desk for payment of fees and distribution of tour schedules.

Primary Program ❖ Preschool to Grade 2

"What's Old, What's New?" ❖ An increased understanding of George Washington's life and times is developed by comparing 18th- and 20th-century objects.

"Setting up Camp" ❖ The children set up camp as a Revolutionary soldier would have, learning about the different artifacts used in the 18th century.

"George Washington's Peruke" ❖ A puppet show featuring a Quaker mouse family living in the Ring house during the time George Washington made his headquarters there.

"Musket Drill" ❖ Using wooden muskets, the children are put through military drills similar to those of the Revolutionary soldier.

"Colonial Toys" ❖ This program focuses on children and toys of the 18th century. The children are invited to demonstrate a Jacob's Ladder, a Buzzer, and a Limber Jack.

Intermediate Program ❖ Grades 3, 4, 5

"A Revolutionary Soldier Dress-Up" ❖ This program focuses on Washington, Lafayette, and the soldiers of the American Army as they prepare for battle. Washington's plans and thoughts before battle, and the soldier's preparation of his musket, will lead the student to consider cause and effect. A student "volunteer soldier" will be outfitted.

"A Quaker Girl Dress-Up" ❖ One of the students is dressed in clothing that would have been worn by a Quaker girl, with a discussion of lifestyles in the 18th century.

"The Losses of Gideon Gilpin" ❖ A play focusing on the impact of the war on the Gilpin family.

"The Dash to Birmingham" ❖ A game format in which the students face and overcome obstacles they might have encountered while fighting the Battle of the Brandywine.

"Which for What" ❖ A seek-and-find exercise, taking place in the museum, in which the children match objects on display with their uses.

Junior High Program

"Read a Letter, Write a Letter" ❖ Students read firsthand accounts of battle events, then write their own letters "home," incorporating writing styles of the 18th century.

"Flags of the American Revolution" ❖ This program teaches the purpose of flags, the history of Revolutionary War flags, and how flags were made in the 18th century. Students will design and construct a flag for a specific Revolutionary War unit.

"Springs and Springhouses" ❖ The springhouse on the Gilpin property was used by the Gilpin family and by Lafayette's servants during his stay. The program emphasizes one method of obtaining water and preserving perishable foods in the 18th century and concludes with time for sketching the hills and springhouse on the Gilpin property.

High School Program

"Magnetic Map" ❖ This unique medium provides a detailed presentation of the Battle of the Brandywine. Causes, strategies, and consequences to both armies and citizens are stressed.

"Early American Medicine—The Soldier's Experience" ❖ This medical history program focuses on the differences in medical procedures and their effectiveness when treating similar wounds of the 18th- and 20th-century soldier.

Traveling Trunk

The Chester County Intermediate Unit's Traveling Trunk Program, **"The Night Before the Battle,"** is available on a reservation basis. There is no charge for the use of the trunk; however, the teacher will be responsible for transporting it to and from the Battlefield. Call the Park to reserve.

Brandywine Battlefield Park is easily accessible via Route 1. Outdoor picnic facilities are available for brown bag lunches. Restroom facilities are available in the Visitor Center. Parking areas are provided at the Visitor Center, historic houses, and picnic areas for both cars and buses.

For reservations or more information call 215 459-3342, or write:

Brandywine Battlefield Park • Box 202 • Chadds Ford, PA 19317

ABOUT US ❖ A Cooperative Effort Brings Best Results

• School tours are available Tuesday through Friday.

• School groups are limited to 60. Special arrangements can be made for larger groups.

• Minimum group of 12 or minimum fee of $36.00.

• One adult chaperone is required for each 10 students.

• Required chaperones and teachers are not charged. Extra chaperones pay student rate.

• All school reservations are confirmed in writing.

• Rain dates are not available.

• To insure a satisfactory experience, it is important to arrive on time.

• Bus or van drivers are expected to transport students from the Visitor Center to the historic houses. Drivers are welcome to join tour groups at no charge.

• No headsets or personal stereos allowed in buildings.

• No eating, drinking, smoking, or gum chewing is permitted in Visitor Center or historic houses.

• Eating facilities include outside picnic tables only.

• Museum gift shop with educational toys and books is available for students, time permitting.

• Bringing siblings is not encouraged. If they attend, the usual student rate will be charged.

School groups not wishing to take advantage of our school programs are welcome to visit the Visitor Center exhibit room.

All school groups planning to picnic and use Park facilities should inform Park personnel in advance.

Check in at the reception desk upon arrival. We will help you keep our picnic areas free of litter by making trash bags available at the desk. Be sure to ask for one!

Thank you for keeping our Park beautiful.

MAKING A RESERVATION

Your day may include a Group Lesson (p. 6), a Private Lesson (p. 7), Outside-In (p.8), an Auditorium Program, a Mini-Show, a natural science film, lunch in The Eatery, and a self-guided tour of exhibits using one of our Museum Safaris. GROUP LESSONS, PRIVATE LESSONS, OUTSIDE-IN, THE EATERY, AND THE AUDITORIUM PROGRAM REQUIRE RESERVATIONS. Mini-Shows and films do not. We recommend that you PLAN all the activities for your class in advance.

RESERVATIONS

Call our reservationists at (215) 299-1060, Monday through Friday, between 9:00 a.m. and 4:00 p.m. Due to the popularity of our programs, we recommend that you call well in advance.

BEFORE YOU CALL

Please be prepared with the following information:

1. Name of teacher accompanying the class
2. Name, mailing address and telephone number of the school
3. Grade level, number of students and number of accompanying adults
4. Preferred date of visit and a second choice
5. Title of each program desired

CONFIRMATION

A confirmation will be sent four weeks prior to your visit. Please read it over carefully. YOU MUST BRING YOUR CONFIRMATION FORM WITH YOU ON YOUR VISIT.

CANCELLATIONS

Cancellations must be made IN WRITING at least TWO WEEKS IN ADVANCE to give another class an opportunity to participate in our programs. A $50 fee per class (40 students or less) will be charged for failure to cancel, in writing, at least two weeks in advance.

FREE TEACHERS' PASS

Get to know us! Look for ideas! Ask for a complimentary Teachers' Pass when you make your reservation. Good for *one* free admision to the Museum.

Please Touch Museum
Pre-Visit Letter to All Adult Chaperones

Your class trip is scheduled for _____

You will be assigned to the following children:
*(the museum requires one adult for every five children
and one adult for every two children with special needs)*

_____

_____

Please stay with your assigned children.
As adult chaperones you are responsible for the children assigned to you. Because the museum is
an open and free environment, please encourage your assigned children to play with activities within one area
where you can always maintain eye contact with them.

When you arrive... While the teacher is at the front
desk making payment arrangements, adult chaperones are asked
to accompany the children assigned to them to a designated coat
area and then into the Museum's Virginia Evans Theater for a
brief orientation about your museum visit. **Self-Guided
Museum Tour...** You and your assigned children may explore
an array of exhibits throughout the entire second floor galleries. It
is suggested you start in an exhibit area where there are few
children. From there you can let your children set the pace and
guide you. Your children may want to quickly explore several
exhibits first and then return to a favorite exhibit for more
focused playing. Your first inclination may be to "see everything", however, sometimes it is more rewarding to explore only
a few exhibits in depth. **Use play as a learning tool...** Because
children learn best when they can discover in hands-on, informal,
and entertaining ways, the Museum's exhibits encourage learning
through playing. Take your cues from the children about what
they find most interesting, then guide and encourage learning
and exploration as the children play.

A Special Focus on the Exhibit, "Foodtastic Journey"
Before the museum visit, your students participated in classroom
activities related to the museum's Foodtastic Journey exhibit.
Foodtastic Journey is an interactive exhibit which enables children to
discover where food comes from. It features three distinct areas: the
farm, the grocery store, the kitchen. **On the Farm, children can
discover how living things need sun, light and nutrients to grow:**
dig potatoes, walk through crops of corn and wheat, pick apples in
an orchard, collect eggs from the chicken coop and milk a cow.
**In the Grocery Store children can discover that one type of food
from the farm can produce many food products:** drive a truckload
of farm products to the store, shop with child-size carts and check out
groceries at real cash registers.
**In the Kitchen children can discover that foods from many groups
can be prepared in healthy ways for a balanced meal:** cook at a
child-size range with a variety of kitchen utensils, stock the shelves
and refridgerator and prepare meals with pictogram recipe cards.

AT THE MUSEUM Parent-Child Activities — Foodtastic Secrets
Prior to your museum visit (the bus ride to the museum may be a good time), give the children one of the following secrets about the
"Foodtastic Journey " exhibit. Ask them to find this secret when they get to the museum.

Please Touch Farm Basket
● When the children find this secret, ask them to carry the
basket through the farm , collecting puzzle pieces along the way.

Corn Stalk Roots
● When the children find this secret, ask them to find the roots of
of the wheat plants and the apple trees. How are the roots the same?

Colored Grocery Shelves
● When the children find this secret, ask them to sort
their groceries by groups of food on these shelves.

Bamboo Vegetable Steamer
● When the children find this secret, ask them to also find the
frying pan. Talk about the different ways of cooking vegetables.

If you have any questions, please contact your group's leader _____ **at** _____

EXPLORER TOUR AT THE PITTSBURGH CHILDREN'S MUSEUM

Welcome to The Pittsburgh Children's Museum. Our philosophy is that a child's work is PLAY! Everyone will want to be and should be INVOLVED.

DESCRIPTION

You have booked an Explorer Tour. This tour is designed to allow a large group to explore all three floors at its own pace. PCM staff are stationed around the Museum to make sure you get the most out of your visit. School chaperons guide their assigned groups from one exhibit to the next. An Explorer Tour is 1 1/2 hours.

IMPORTANT TIPS

1. Please be on time. We are not able to extend your tour time or admit your class early.

2. Bring the recommended adult to child ratio. The Museum Sampler ratio is 1 adult per 5 children. Please have these groups arranged before coming to the Museum.

3. Wear name tags. We like to know who we are talking to.

4. Visit restrooms and gift shop throughout your visit. Do not wait until the very end of your visit, both areas are too small to accommodate large numbers.

5. Adults, please plan on guiding your assigned group from one exhibit to the next. Museum staff will be on hand to explain the exhibits and assist you. However, you must lead the way!

6. Enjoy yourselves. These exhibits are favorites: Silk Screen Studio, Stuffee demonstration, Luckey's Climber, the Puppet Floor, and Looking at You.

7. Please note: You may not get to spend as much time in each area as your group might want. You may choose to spend more time in one area which means less time in another. This is not a bad choice - each group's interests and needs are different. Your choices will reflect this.

FINDING PHILADELPHIA'S PAST: Visions and Revisions

Greetings!

We look forward to your upcoming visit to FINDING PHILADELPHIA'S PAST at the Historical Society of Pennsylvania. You and your students will get the most out of this trip if you prepare them for what they will see and do during their visit. To help you prepare them, we have enclosed an easily reproducible lotto-like game which introduces words, objects, and ideas that will be discussed. At your request, we can also send you a colorful, high tech six minute introductory video to the exhibition which you can return the day of your visit.

Upon arrival at the Historical Society, please ask the guard at the front desk to notify the Education Department. If you are paying for the lesson, give your check or cash to a representative of the Education Department, not the person at the front desk. We can provide you with a receipt. As you enter, you will see a small gift shop on your right. If students wish to purchase items they will have to go in groups of five at the end of the lesson.

Our lessons have many types of activities which may include a scavenger hunt, role playing, writing, doing a craft, deciphering old handwriting, and public speaking. Your students will work individually, in pairs, and in small groups of 4-5 during the lesson. We need you to decide in advance which combination of students will work most productively in pairs and small groups. We will need your assistance throughout the lesson to keep your students on task and to alert us to students who need extra assistance. There is always some part of the lesson that needs completion upon your return to school. We find that when students know that their museum visit is part of their school experience, they take it more seriously.

Because FINDING PHILADELPHIA'S PAST has many objects at a level and distance easy for young people to see, it is imperative that students understand that touching can only be done with the eyes and brain, not hands and feet. We reserve the right to ask any unruly students to leave the exhibit. Please be prepared to have someone stay with this student in another room. We will provide an activity for that student.

At the conclusion of the lesson we will give you an evaluation form for you and your students to complete. We are anxious to make our lessons as interesting as possible which only can be done with you help.

Thank you for choosing to bring your class to FINDING PHILADELPHIA'S PAST.

Sincerely,

Cynthia Little and Kate Stover

HISTORICAL SOCIETY OF PENNSYLVANIA Education Department

1300 Locust Street   Philadelphia, PA 19107   (215) 732-6201

FINDING PHILADELPHIA'S PAST: Visions and Revisions

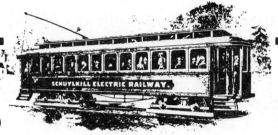

SCHOOL GROUP CONFIRMATION FORM

Date of Visit_____   Cost _____

Time_____

Lesson_____

Number in Group_____   Age/Grade_____

School_____

Contact Person_____

     Phone _____

     Address_____

_____

_____

_____

Lunch at Society: yes / no

Special Needs_____

_____

_____

_____

Please notify us in advance of any changes in your plans.

The Society does have a gift shop which students will see as they enter the building. If you plan for them to visit the shop after their lesson or tour, arrange for them to go in groups of no more than five.

Thank you for visiting FINDING PHILADELPHIA'S PAST: Visions and Revisions. We look forward to meeting you in the near future.

Cynthia Little
Kate F. Stover
Jacqueline Hawkins

HISTORICAL SOCIETY OF PENNSYLVANIA   Education Department

1300 Locust Street   Philadelphia, PA 19107   (215) 732-6201

CHESTER COUNTY HISTORICAL SOCIETY

A Face to Remember

Before there were cameras, people often had their portraits painted. They, of course, wanted to look their very best.

Select a portrait in the gallery and try the following game. Study the painting very carefully for 60 seconds. Then turn away and have someone ask you the following questions:

1. What words would you use to describe the person's mood? (happy, sad, serious, thoughtful, etc.)

2. What is the person wearing?

3. Is she/he wearing a hat? a wig? anything on his/her head?

4. Is she/he wearing glasses?

5. Is she/he wearing any jewelry?

6. Is the person standing or sitting? Can you take the person's pose?

7. Is the person inside a building or outside?

8. What else is in the picture?

When you have answered the questions, turn around and check how well you remembered.

Now draw your portrait the way you would like to be seen.

What special object would you like to hold in your hands?

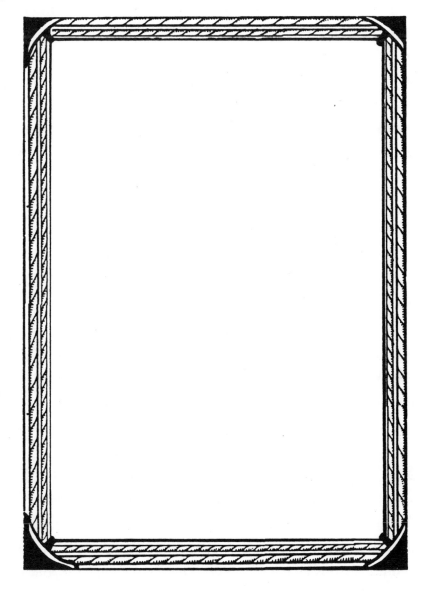

The University Museum of Archaeology & Anthropology

FUN FACTS:
THE RAVEN'S JOURNEY GALLERY

INTRODUCTION:

Have you ever put together a puzzle? If you're like most people you probably try to put the straight edge pieces together first so that you can have a frame for the rest of the picture. Perhaps you join the rest of the pieces by matching shapes and colors together and by using the picture on top of the box. You probably have to try several pieces together before you find the proper match.

Trying to build a picture of an ancient culture is similar to putting together a picture from a mound of puzzle pieces. That is what anthropologists and archaeologists do: they try to match pieces of information about people and their way of life to give us a picture of what those folks were like. Only they do not have the finished picture on top of the puzzle box to guide them. What they do know, though, is some of the basic things that we also know about ourselves. To name a few: we live and we die, we eat and drink, we need protection from the environment, we have relationships with our family and friends, we have a way of communicating with each other, we like and value certain things, we are afraid and suspicious of other things, and so on. A lot of anthropologists' and archaeologists' work is putting many ideas together to try and develop an accurate picture of a culture. This can take years.

What you will see in the gallery is an assortment of the puzzle pieces that archaeologists and anthropologists have worked with to discover something about the way of life and people of a particular culture. Try to imagine that you are an anthropologist or archaeologist putting together a picture of how people lived with these pieces. What do you think you would need to know in order to do this? Think of some questions you could ask to get this information. Your museum tour guide is someone who can help you answer those questions. Use your tour guide as you might use a picture on the top of the puzzle box to get as much information as you can about the pieces and how they were discovered and put together. Come prepared with some questions to ask. Until your tour, here are some fun facts to help you get started.....

BACKGROUND ON THE RAVEN'S JOURNEY GALLERY:

This gallery looks at the world of Alaska's Native people: the Athapaskan, Tlingit and Eskimo. All of these people believed that people, animals, and objects have spirits. One of the most important spirits was the bird, Raven. There are many stories about Raven, the tricks he played and the lessons he taught. When you visit the gallery your guide can tell you more about him.

The collection has items or artifacts (as they are called in a museum), that were collected within the last 125 years. The collectors obtained these artifacts when they lived in these communities. They observed and asked questions concerning daily life, important ceremonies, and how these objects were used.

SOME IMPORTANT WORDS TO LOOK UP AND LEARN:

AMULET
ATHAPASKAN
CLAN
ESKIMO
FETISH
IVORY
KAYAK
POTLATCH
QUILLING
TLINGIT
TOTEM

SOME FUN FACTS:

1) The Native people of Alaska used fishskin to make jackets and bags. Why do you think they chose fishskin? Look for the clothing made of fishskin when you visit the gallery.

2) The Eskimo had a winter home and a summer home. Why do you think they needed two houses? Your guide will be happy to give you more information about the different houses.

3) The Tlingit and Athapaskan peoples made a canoe by hollowing out a single tree. How long do you think it would take you to carve a canoe out of a tree?

4) Several Tlingit families shared the same one room house. They separated their sleeping quarters with a screen. Everybody would cook, eat and play together. Look for the beautifully decorated screen when you come visit the gallery.

5) The Tlingit and Athapaskan people celebrated a special ceremony called the Potlatch. In order to impress their friends, with how rich and important they were, people giving the Potlatch gave away all of their possessions and even threw some into the water. What are some things you do to impress your friends? Ask your guide to tell you more about the Potlatch.

6) Northwest Coast peoples put designs all over their faces. Some people put rings through their noses or lips and placed large spools in their earlobes to make them longer. Look for all of these items in the gallery. What are some things you do to make yourself more attractive?

Follow
THE DINOSAUR TRAIL
at Dinosaurs Alive!

Use the exhibits to help you draw the missing parts of the dinosaurs and *Dimetrodon*. The questions will also help you look at the exhibits. (Answers are at the end.)

The Carnegie Museum of Natural History
August 11 - October 28, 1990

Stegosaurus

1. Look at the head of *Stegosaurus*. Was its brain as big as yours? _____

2. How many people could have ridden on the back of *Stegosaurus*? _____

Allosaurus

3. This creature was totally awesome. Did it eat plants or meat? _____

4. Name two ways in which the front feet of *Allosaurus* were different from its hind feet? (Look at the back of the foot.)

_____

_____

Name _____

Artifact Detectives

Make a quick sketch of the artifact.

List some words which describe the artifact. _____

_____

What color is it? _____

What materials is it made of? _____

Is any part of it missing? _____ If yes, what? _____

Was it hand made or machine made? _____

What type of the person made it? _____

Where was it made? _____

When was it made? 200 or more years ago, about 100 years ago, in this century

How might this artifact have been used? What makes you think so?

_____

_____

ATWATER ★ KENT ★ MUSEUM
THE HISTORY MUSEUM OF PHILADELPHIA

Symbols of a New Nations

A **symbol** is a picture that stands for an idea, story or feeling. For example, a picture of a heart is often a **symbol** for love. After the American Revolution, America no longer wanted to use English **symbols**. They wanted to create their own **symbols** for their new country. Below are three **symbols** that were very popular in American art in the late 1700s and early 1800s.

Although each **symbol** may vary in its size, shape, or detail, a version of each one below can be found at least 4 times in these two galleries. On the lines beside each **symbol**, make a list of the objects where you have found the **symbol**.

1. _____

2. _____

3. _____

4. _____

The Eagle: a symbol of freedom

1. _____

2. _____

3. _____

4. _____

**Fruit: a symbol of the land
and its bounty**

1. _____

2. _____

3. _____

4. _____

**Columns: a symbol of democracy
and strength**

Turn to the back of this page to **learn** more about these symbols.

— Philadelphia Museum of Art School Program

GALLERY GAME:
DETAIL DETECTIVE

Select an object from the ARCHITECT + ARTIFACTS exhibition which uses one of the following building systems in its design:

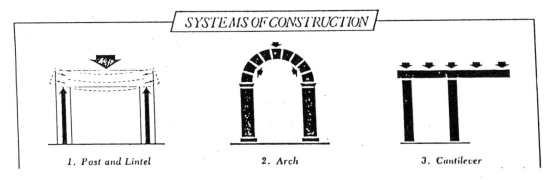

Pretend you have a magnifying glass, and enlarge JUST A PART of the object you have selected. Draw it here:

Now trade with a friend. Find the objects each of you have drawn.

— FROM *TEACHER'S GUIDE*, "ARCHITECTS & ARTIFACTS," THE SOCIETY FOR ART IN CRAFTS, PITTSBURGH

Quaker Visions Word Scramble

Instructions: Unscramble the word in bold print to complete the sentence.

Name: _____

1). The original plan for Philadelphia was laid out on a _____ (**irdg**) which consists of straight lines crossing to make boxes.

2). The Lenni Lenape _____ (**dsnaini**) were already living in the Delaware Valley when Europeans arrived.

3). _____ (**mialilw nepn**) was a Quaker and the owner and proprietor of Pennsylvania.

4). A member of the religious Society of Friends is known as a _____ _____ (**kruqea**).

5). A _____ (**yevrours**) examines the form and size of an area of land and makes a map.

6). William Penn had a _____ (**nsoiiv**) of Philadelphia, or a clear picture of the city's future.

7). The Indians made _____ (**muapwm**) which are beads made from shells.

8). _____ (**gtoamineri**) is when people leave their homeland to live somewhere else.

9). Philadelphia was planned to stretch between the _____ (**ewlaadre**) river to the east and the _____ (**yklulihls**) river to the west.

10). Pennsylvania was a _____ (**ptiyarpror**) colony, given to William Penn by the King of England as payment for a debt.

etail Detectives

SHAKER FURNITURE

Shakers were religious people who lived together in groups around America from the late 1700's to the mid-1900's. They grew their own food and made their own buildings, furniture, clothes and tools. Everthing they made was simple and useful, for they believed that fancy things only led to greed and took their attention away from God. "Simple" does not mean ugly. The Shakers made objects with beautiful shapes, lines and materials. Look at the 6 clues below and try to find the objects they describe. Numbers 1, 2, 3 and 4 are in the glass cases. Numbers 5 and 6 are in the Shaker bedroom.

1

The letters on this <u>towel</u> aren't initials to a name.
A Shaker wouldn't brag or boast or want that kind of fame
"B" stands for "believers," "visitors" is "V."
The guests who stayed with Shakers found warm hospitality.

2

<u>Baskets</u> by Shakers
are made without flaw
of hickory, ash, oak, and rye straw.
Find one that is woven
so straight and so tight
that between all the pieces
there's no space in sight.

3

Among the talents
of the Shakers
Was their skill as <u>furniture</u> makers.
Just look how cherry wood became
<u>three legs</u> whose curves
are exactly the same.

4

Did you know that wood can bend?
Here's an <u>oval</u>
find its end.
<u>Boxes</u> were made
both big and small.
Can you find one?
Can you find all?

5

No fancy velvet or special gold tacks.
Just a <u>seat</u> and four legs
and a straight <u>wooden back</u>.
A <u>chair</u> is to sit in
and that's about all.
So when it's not used,
it can hang on the wall.

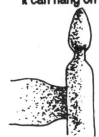

6

<u>Down near the floor</u>
where a Shaker once stood
you'll find this neat pattern
of <u>holes in the wood</u>.
These holes form a vent
lets fresh air pass through
and keeps all the rooms
smelling clean, fresh and new.

ATWATER ★ KENT ★ MUSEUM
THE HISTORY MUSEUM OF PHILADELPHIA
5 SOUTH 7TH STREET, PHILADELPHIA, PA 19106 MU6-363

THE CITY BENEATH US: Suggested Classroom Activities

Lesson Description: Artifacts from the City Archaeological Collection enable students to unravel clues about Philadelphia's past. A discussion of archaeological methods will be included.

Pre-Visit: Excavate your classroom's trash can (on a relatively clean day). Take out one object at a time, identify it, list it, sketch it and continue until the can is empty. The list of items should progress from newly discarded to earlier discards, illustrating the basic archaeological theory that the newest material is on the top and the oldest is on the bottom. List the types of materials found in the trash can, and discuss which if any objects would be likely to survive 100 years. Try to reconstruct the classroom environment and activities using only the information learned from the trash can. This exercise will illustrate that most archaeologists have only a partial view of the society they study.

For a variation on this activity, excavate the trash can of a neighboring classroom. Students should act as detectives, trying to determine the source of the trash can and the activities of the students in that room.

Discuss the types of information that can be learned from a trash can. What can be discovered about people's everyday lives (food, clothing, work, leisure pursuits, etc.)?

Post-Visit: Ask students to choose objects that they consider to be important in their everyday lives. Students should then imagine themselves as archaeologists of the future discovering all or part of these objects. What will the object itself tell future generations about each student, and about life in the 20th-century?

Looking for a
quick and easy way
to prepare
your students
for their
museum visit?

Pre- and Post-Visit Activities For Your Classroom featuring the exhibit, *Step Into Art*

Especially For Teachers…

Please Touch Museum

Pre- and Post-Visit Classroom Activities

- **Junk Art** Use old toys and household junk to create mini-sculptures. Examples include: bathroom tissue tubes, egg cartons, fabric scraps, buttons, packing peanuts and old toy trinkets affixed together with white glue.

- **Shape Art** Create shape pictures using paper and fabric shapes. Examples include: circles, squares and triangles glued together to make a favorite scene, or open-ended shapes glued together in a collage design.

- **Shadow Play Art** Use familiar finger play songs and stories (such as "eensy-weensy spider") or shadow puppet props (made from cardboard shapes affixed to popsicle sticks) to create shadows on your classroom wall. To add color to your shadows, shine flashlights covered with colored cellophane.

- **Stained Glass Window Art** Create a "stained glass" collage by gluing colored cellophane shapes to a clear plastic paper or by gluing colored tissue paper shapes together. Explore blending colors by overlapping the cellophane or tissue paper. Finish with a construction paper frame and display your creations in a classroom window.

- **Peek-a-Boo** Play peek-a-boo with textured art by affixing different textured shapes to a large piece of paper. Cover each shape with a mini paper door. Or make paper envelopes and affix to a large piece of paper. Hide different textured shapes inside the envelopes. Make small holes in the envelopes and encourage peeking at the different textures inside.

- **Texture Art Walk** Hunt for textures you can see and feel as you take either an indoor or outdoor art walk. Keep a log book of the textures you find and share it with your children at circle time after your walk.

Teacher Tips

- Look for the special pieces of junk the artist used to make the elephant's trunk, ears, tusks, mouth and tail.

- Look for the photographs of the artist making **Artie**.

- Look for the fabric applique art works that use many little shapes to make a big village scene.

- Look for the colored lights in **Shadow Play** and encourage children to cast shadows on the wall.

- Look for the painting of boats moving down a river and encourage your children to draw squiggly lines on their paper. Then watch the line move "like water" inside the zoetrope.

- Sing the "eensy-weensy spider" as you move your fingers up the wall like a spider casting colored shadows.

- Look for the stained glass window and encourage children to make their own "stained glass" design.

- Look inside and outside of the special peepholes on the **Space Geode's** surface.

- Look for the feely-rocks near the wall and encourage children to talk about the textures they feel inside.

- Look for the mask with the deerhide and armadillo skin decorations.

- Look at the painting and talk about the textures you can see and feel.

Vocabulary

AFTERLIFE. Existence after death. The ancient Egyptians believed the perfect afterlife was an idealized version of their earthly existence.

AMULET. Good luck charm. Many represented gods or goddesses or their symbols. Others were hieroglyphs that stood for protective words such as life, good, beauty, and stability. By wearing such charms, the owner received the powers associated with the deity or hieroglyph.

ANOINT. To rub with a perfumed oil or ointment.

ARCHAEOLOGICAL EVIDENCE. The material remains of past human societies, studied by scientists called archaeologists.

"BOOK OF THE DEAD." A New Kingdom collection of spells often written on papyrus or linen and placed in the tomb with the mummy to give it protection in its journey to the afterlife. It was actually called the "Chapters of Coming Forth by Day."

CANOPIC JARS. Four jars that contained the deceased's lungs, liver, intestines, and stomach. They were buried with the mummy in the tomb.

CATARACT. A stretch of rapids interrupting the flow of the Nile, caused by boulders of granite interspersed in the Nubian sandstone belt.

CLAPPERS. A musical instrument consisting of two sticks tied together and played like castanets.

CROOK AND FLAIL. Symbols of kingship. The crook is a shepherd's staff with a hook at the upper end; the flail is a free-swinging stick tied to the end of a long handle.

CULT. A system of religious worship or ritual.

DELTA. A usually triangular deposit of silt at the mouth of a river where it flows into a sea or ocean.

HEADREST. A support for the head of a person sleeping on his or her side. It consisted of a curved portion, which held the head, on a pedestal about the height of the shoulder.

IBIS. A large, heron-like, wading bird with long legs and a long, slender, curved bill.

INUNDATION. The annual flood of the Nile River that occurred in ancient times from June to early October. It was caused by rains in Central Africa and melting snow and rains in the Ethiopian highlands.

LOTUS. A form of water lily that bears a showy flower. It was a symbol of Upper Egypt.

LOWER EGYPT. The area of Egypt consisting of the Nile River's fan-shaped delta. The Nile flows north through Lower Egypt into the Mediterranean Sea.

MASTABAS. Early tombs built of mud brick or stone in a rectangular shape at ground level with a burial chamber below ground.

MORTUARY TEMPLE. A structure where the dead were prepared for burial and worshiped.

MUMMY. The preserved corpse of an ancient Egyptian.

MYRRH. A fragrant, bitter-tasting gum resin exuded from several varieties of trees in east Africa and the Arabian peninsula, used in making incense and perfume.

A READING LIST FOR SCHOOL CHILDREN PLANNING TO VISIT
QUIET VALLEY LIVING HISTORICAL FARM

IF YOU LIVED IN COLONIAL TIMES, Ann McGovern, The Four Winds
    Press

A B C BOOK OF EARLY AMERICANA, Eric Sloan, Doubleday & Co.

CHARLIE NEEDS A CLOAK, Tomie dePaola, Prentice-Hall, Inc.

PELLE'S NEW SUIT, Elpha Beshow, Delacorte

HOW A SHIRT GREW IN THE FIELD, K. Ushinsky, McGraw Hill Book
    Co.

LITTLE BRITCHES, Ralph Moody, Norton

DIARY OF AN EARLY AMERICAN BOY, Eric Sloan, Funk.

ABE LINCOLN GETS HIS CHANCE, Frances Cavanah, Scholastic.

THE STORY OF BEN FRANKLIN, Eve Merriam, Scholastic.

JIM BECKWOURTH, NEGRO MOUNTAIN MAN, Harold W. Felton,
    Apollo.

....IF YOU GREW UP WITH ABRAHAM LINCOLN, Ann McGovern
    Scholastic.

CHARLOTTE'S WEB, E. B. White, Dell.

A SPECIAL BRAVERY, Johanna Sohnston, Apollo

TWO IN THE WILDERNESS, Mary Thompson, Scholastic.

THE STORY OF JOHNNY APPLESEED, Aliki, Prentice Hall.

JOHNNY APPLESEED, Eve Moore, Scholastic.

TROUBLE RIVER, Betsy Byans, Seafarer.

THE CHILDREN WHO STAYED ALONE, Bonnie Bess Worline,
    Scholastic

THY FRIEND OBADIAH, Brinton Turkle, Seafarer.

FLIGHT TO FREEDOM, Henritta Buchmaster, Dell.

BLUE RIDGE BILLY, Lois Lensky, Dell.

CAPTURED BY THE MOHAWKS, Sterling North, Dell.

BREAD AND BUTTER INDIAN, Anne Colver, Camelot.

Fabled Family Members

Look for myths and heroes on your family tree.

Ask an older adult at home these questions to discover hidden family heroes and the beliefs your family treasures.

❑ How did members of your family make a living? What training did they have to have for their jobs? What were job conditions like?

❑ What members of the family served in the military? What were their duties? Did any see active service? What war? Where? What stories have been told about their experiences?

❑ What stories have you hear about how hard their work was or of things that happened at work?

❑ How did wars affect the lives of others in the family?

❑ What were the responsibilities of the woman of the house? What jobs, if any, did women hold outside the home? How did they manage to do both?

❑ Who in your family has come through really tough times? What is their story?

❑ What big events occurred in the life of your family or your town? What stories are told of natural disasters like floods, tornados, blizzards, etc.?

❑ Who are the "pioneers" in your family—the first people in the family to do or accomplish something? What is their story?

❑ What family stories have been told about good times or hard times?

❑ Who do you admire most in the family? Why?

❑ What stories has your family told of great fortunes made or lost? Are they funny or sad?

❑ Who is your hero outside the family? Why?

—PITTSBURGH CHILDREN'S MUSEUM

A MYTH FOR ME

Who—real or imaginary—would you like to add to the Myth gallery?
Your art work can hang in the museum along with Andy Warhol's!

■ **Think** about someone who stands for a set of ideas or beliefs that you believe in.

■ **Draw** his, her, or its picture in Pop Art style.

■ **Write:**

  • the name of your character;
  • the myth he, she, or it stands for;
  • why he, she, or it should be added to Myths.

■ **Send** your Myth nomination to:
  The Pittsburgh Children's Museum
  One Landmarks Square
  Pittsburgh, PA 15212

Visit your drawing in the gallery for four weeks after your nomination arrives.

The name of my myth character:

My myth stands for these ideas and beliefs:

My myth should be added to the Myths gallery because

My name and hometown:

POST-LESSON PHOTOGRAPHIC WORKSHEET

ACTIVITY 1

You are an investigator for the U.S. Department of Labor. Using
the photograph on the newspaper have each student complete the
report.

Investigator's Report

Task Force No. _____

Reporter _____

    1. Is the work area safe for workers?

    2. Is the lighting adequate?

    3. Would you recommend that workers wear protective
       clothing? If so, what?

    4. Should there be a minimum age limit for this task?
       If so, recommend an appropriate age.

    5. Would you recommend that the children in the photo-
       graph be allowed to continue to work at that job?
       Why or why not?

ASK THE ARTIST

Name _____

Cultural background _____

Craft tradition _____

Profession _____

Find the following information by observing or talking with the artist:

What are the processes, skills, and materials involved in doing this craft?

What is the origin of the craft? What is the craft's importance to its culture or community?

How has the tradition been passed along? How did the artist learn the craft?

What is the importance of the craft to the artist? to the culture or community?

How is quality judged in this craft tradition? What makes a piece "good"?

The Pittsburgh Children's Museum Outreach program recently came to your school. We hope you enjoyed it! We would appreciate it if you would take the time to answer a few questions about the presentation, and to have a teacher from each grade level that saw it to do the same. Feedback from principals, teachers and parents is invaluable in the evaluation, planning and development of the Children's Museum programming

Thank you for your cooperation.

Lois Winslow
Education/Outreach Coordinator

NAME:_____

POSITION:_____ IF TEACHER, GRADE LEVEL:_____
          (Principal, Teacher, Parent)

NAME OF SCHOOL:_____ SCHOOL DISTRICT:_____

NAME & DATE OF PROGRAM:_____ __/ /__

1. How would you rate the overall impact of the presentation?
    _____Excellent_____Good_____Fair_____Poor

2. Was the presentation relevent to your curriculum and/or classroom
    presentation?
    _____Yes_____No

3. How would you rate this presentation as a program generating
    interest in your course of study?
    _____Excellent_____Good_____Fair_____Poor

4. Did students discuss content of the program in the classroom?
    _____Yes_____No

5. Would you have this program again next year?
    _____Yes_____No(if no, why?)_____

6. Have you been to The Pittsburgh Children's Museum?
    _____Yes (with class) _____ Yes (with family) _____No

The Pittsburgh Children's Museum

One Landmarks Square
Allegheny Center
Pittsburgh, Pennsylvania 15212

(412) 322-5059

7. Would you recommend this program to others?
   _____Yes_____No (if no, why?)_____

8. Would you book other outreach programs from the Children's Museum?
   _____Yes_____No (if no, why?)_____
   Which?_____

9. Knowing that the Children's Museum directs its programming for preschool children through age twelve, would you take a field trip to the Children's Museum?
   _____Yes_____No (if no, why?)_____

10. What other kind of outreach programming from the Children's Museum would you like to see offered?_____
    _____

    COMMENTS:

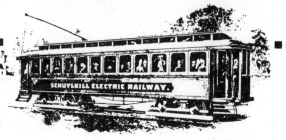

FINDING PHILADELPHIA'S PAST: Visions and Revisions

EVALUATION FORM

Please take a few minutes to complete this form and return it to us in the attached envelope. Your input will help us to continually evaluate and improve our lessons.

1) What was the title of the lesson you had today?

_____

2) What were the strengths of this lesson?

_____
_____
_____
_____

3) What were the weaknesses of this lesson? How could this lesson have been improved?

_____
_____
_____
_____

4) Was the level of difficulty of the lesson appropriate for your school group? If not, explain.

_____
_____
_____
_____

5) Would you be interested in coming back for another lesson?

_____

6) If possible, please include some comments from your students. We would like to get their feedback as well!

_____
_____
_____
_____

HISTORICAL SOCIETY OF PENNSYLVANIA   Education Department

1300 Locust Street   Philadelphia, PA 19107   (215) 732-6201

Museum on the Move

A Program of
Carnegie Museum of Natural History,
Carnegie Institute

Go To
The Source

Secondary-level resource materials
for the study of primary sources
and local history
from the
Historical Society of York County

TROUPERS
In-School
Artifacts
Programs

ART
you can
touch

from the
Allentown
Art Museum

Please Touch Museum To Go! Traveling Trunks

The Arts ◆◆◆◆◆◆

Art Alive: Fine Art for Kids
Explore exciting art themes in two trunks.

Art Around the World
The Americas: Native America, Mexico, Central & South America
Africa and Ancient Egypt
The East: Japan, China, India, the Middle East and Southeast Asia

Circus
Create your own Big Top with costumes, music, games and more.

Happily Ever After: Folklore and Fairy Tales
Make believe with puppetry, games, costumes, books and tapes.

Museum in a Trunk
Sample exhibits and collections found at Please Touch Museum through costumes, artifacts, activities and models.

Make-and-Take Trunk: Please Touch Museum will custom design your very own trunk for a fair or company picnic! You provide the adult help and we create an educational and fun art activity for young children that they can make at your event and take home. All supplies are included in this trunk in addition to activity directions for your adult help.

Sciences ▼▼▼▼▼▼

Bugs! And Other Amazing Insects
Discover the incredible world of insects through scientific investigation. Includes a companion box of "careful touch" specimens

Dinosaurs
Travel back to prehistoric times and learn about discovering and naming dinosaurs, plus lots of dino fun!

Food: From Farm to Market to Table
Follow the journey food takes from the farm to the grocery store and finally into your kitchen.

Math: 1, 2, 3 Go!
Approach math concepts in a fun way. Let's sort, measure, count and play games.

The Seasons
Explore summer, fall, winter, and spring and how people, plants and animals change and adapt to the seasons.

Space
Learn about the solar system and our planet Earth through an investigation of astronauts and space travel.

Transportation: Wings & Wheels
Compare old, new and different forms of travel from school bus to space ships!

Water Animals
Find out about water as a home and what creatures are found there.

Your Body: Making Healthy Choices
Learn about nutrition, simple anatomy and keeping our bodies healthy.

Social Sciences ●●●●●

Take your children on an exciting journey that helps them to understand the many different cultures that make up the world. Explore authentic artifacts, dress and musical instruments, family life and geography.
African-American Experience
China
Head-to-Toe (Mexico, the Netherlands, Nigeria and China)
India
Native Americans
Poland
Puerto Rico

Franklin's Philadelphia
Discover what it was like to be a child in Philadelphia in the 1700s.

Geography: From your Neighborhood to the World
Learn about your environment and the world through map-making and charting, stories and art activities.

Red, White & Blue
Celebrate patriotism and citizenship in the United States through its symbols, heroes and leaders.

You Can Be: Careers
Explore the many choices available in the working world. How do the unique interests of people lead to their career choices?

Traveling Trunk Rentals and Programs
● Schools ◆ Hospitals ▲ Camps ●

Trunk Rentals
2-Week Rental	$ 60.00
3-Week Rental	$ 85.00
4-Week Rental	$100.00

Make-and-Take Traveling Trunk
	$125.00

Includes activity, supplies, PTM signs, suggestions for your adult help and 1-Week Rental.
Pick-up and return of Traveling Trunks is the responsibility of the renter.

Outreach Programs
1-Hour Traveling Trunk Program by museum staff	$150.00
2 Programs at same location	$250.00

Rental and Outreach Combinations
1-Hour Traveling Trunk "Grand Opening" Program by museum staff plus 2-Week Rental	$200.00
2 Programs at same site plus 2-Week Rental	$300.00

Trunk return after rental is the responsibility of the renter.

Note: We encourage the renter who will be sharing the trunks with more than one or two classrooms to consider a longer rental time, a minimum of one week per class.
A checklist of items in the trunk is provided with each rental. Any items needing replacement will be billed to the renter.

Payment is due two weeks prior to your program or rental.
Museum members receive a 10% discount on Traveling Trunk rentals.

Further Information call
215-963-0667

Please Touch ■ Museum To Go! ▲ Traveling Trunks

WHAT YOU CAN BORROW:

A teacher may borrow one boxed kit at a time for a three-week period. An enclosed Teacher's Guide includes support material about The Society, the American Craft Movement, the artist, and the object as well as suggestions for use. Some kits also contain related slides and cassette tapes.

HOW TO REGISTER

Registration is by school building. Payment of an annual $25.00 fee (Sept/June), and the completion of a registration form requiring the principal's signature grant unlimited borrowing privileges to all teachers assigned to a registered building.

ARRANGING A LOAN

To reserve a loan, please ask for the Director of Education at (412) 261-7003, Monday through Friday between 9:00 A.M. and 5:00 P.M.or write:

    Educational Loan Collection
    The Society for Art in Crafts
    2100 Smallman Street
    Pittsburgh, PA 15222

PICKING UP AND RETURNING LOAN

Loans are picked up and returned to The Society for Art in Crafts in Pittsburgh's Strip District by a teacher or a school representative.

Business hours ONLY:
    Monday-Friday, 9 A.M. - 5 P.M.
    Saturday 10 A.M. - 5 P.M.
    Sunday 1 P.M. - 4 P.M.

EDUCATIONAL LOAN COLLECTION:

VISUAL CATALOGUE

THE SOCIETY FOR ART IN CRAFTS

Or We'll Come to You...

Assembly Programs

(theater-style productions)

Terminal Cafe

Concerned with the many issues facing the global environment, this fun and informative musical production discusses the importance of environmental responsibility. Recycling, proper waste disposal and conservation are but a few of the messages relayed. Study guide.

Running time: 40 minutes
Cost: $375 first program; $200 each additional (same day/location) Accommodates up to 250, K - 6

Joe Magarac: Man of Steel

The era of Pittsburgh's Steel Industry was a fascinating time. Take a look at our city's past through the mythical legend, Joe Magarac. Brothers Tim and Bob Hartman are a hilarious duo as they bring Pittsburgh's past to life. Study Guide.

Running time: 50 minutes
Cost: $350 first program; $200 each additional (same day/location) Accommodates up to 250, K - 6

Construct-a-Tale

Character, conflict and setting: these are the basic building blocks of a good story. Using examples from folktales from around the world, the Hartman brothers vividly share their skills as actors, comedians and storytellers. The Hartmans embellish their performance with input from the audience, keeping students thoroughly entertained as they help them recognize the key to clear expression. Study guide.

Running time: 45 minutes
Cost: $350 first program; $200 each additional (same day/location) Accommodates up to 250, 1 - 6

Puppet Shows

The Sword in the Pork Barrel

Arthurian legend will never be the same as resident puppeteer Charlie Holden (of We're Holden Puppets) and partner, Laura Opshinsky, present an unforgettable cast of puppets in this light-hearted salute to the Middle Ages. Study Guide.

Running time: 45 minutes
Cost: $400 first program; $250 each additional (same day/location) Accommodates up to 200, K - 6

Tales of Hotei

Hotei, a free-spirited monk from ancient Japan shares whimsical words of wisdom based on Japanese legend. Puppeteer Charlie Holden incorporates unusual forms of Japanese puppetry to tell the tale. Show includes discussion and explanations of the puppets.

Running time: 45 minutes
Cost: $375 first program; $215 each additional (same day/location) Accommodates up to 200, K - 6

Bearly Spring

Join Buddy Bear as he wakes from hibernation and learns the essentials of self-esteem from his furry forest friends.

Running time: 45 minutes
Cost: $350 first program; $200 each additional (same day/location) Accommodates up to 200, Pre - 4

RESOURCES FOR TEACHERS

Look for Newspapers-in-Education supplement "Thomas Eakins" in the *Daily News*.

EVENINGS FOR EDUCATORS
WEDNESDAYS 4:00 - 5:30 P.M.

Become familiar with our various school programs in an informal setting. Museum education staff members are available to answer questions, schedule tours, or talk about other programs and exhibits. Evenings for Educators are open free of charge. Reservations are suggested, please call the Department of Museum Education, 972-7608.

September 11 **Telling Tales** (grades pre-K - 12)

October 2 **Thomas Eakins** (grades 9 - 12)

October 9 **Now Showing** Preview of all programs available

February 5 **Now Showing** Preview of all programs available

CONFERENCE FOR ARTISTS AND ARTIST-TEACHERS

The Education of the Artist: 100 Years of Exploration
SATURDAY, OCTOBER 12, 10:00 A.M. - 4:00 P.M.

Join nationally-recognized art educators and art historians Diana Korzenik, Brent Wilson, Maria Chamberlin-Hellman, and Ronald Onorato as they examine the training of 19th and 20th c. American artists. Participate in provocative break-out sessions led by area arts educators exploring current art teaching in the Philadelphia area and national movements which inform practice.

Conference fee: $20, includes lunch and program materials. Add $9 per discount ticket and join us for the 8:00 p.m. premiere of **Marks on the Water**, a play about Philadelphia's leading 19th c. art educator, Thomas Eakins. The conference is supported by a grant from The Dietrich Foundation.

SATURDAY WORKSHOPS FOR EDUCATORS

Workshops for art and classroom teachers help effectively prepare students for a field trip to the museum. Sessions include gallery demonstrations, scholarly lectures, and suggestions of ways to integrate the subject matter into the art and general curriculum through group discussion and hands-on classroom activities. In-service credit is available through the Montgomery County IU-23 for any combination of 15 hours of participation.

There will be a $5.00 fee for materials and texts which will become the property of the participant. The fee is payable to *The Pennsylvania Academy of the Fine Arts*.

The Stories in Art, The Art of Stories
October 19, 9:00 a.m. - 2:00 p.m.
for teachers grades K - 12.

Thomas Eakins Rediscovered
November 9, 9:00 a.m. - 1:00 p.m.
* open to teachers grades 7 through 12 only

Art and Architecture
November 23, 9:00 a.m. - 1:00 p.m.
for teachers grades 3 - 12.

The Stories in Art, The Art of Stories
February 1, 1992, 9:00 a.m. - 1:00 p.m.
for teachers grades K - 12.

Art for Non-Art Teachers
March 21, 1992 9:00 a.m. - 1:00 p.m.
* open to teachers pre-school through grade 6

FREE FALL LECTURES

Pennsylvania Folk Legends Dr. Kenneth Thigpen, Associate Professor of English and American Studies, Penn State University
Saturday, October 19, 1:00 - 2:00 p.m.

Humor and Disaster in the Folk Tales and True Stories of Rural Pennsylvania
Dr. James Y. Glimm, Professor of English, Mansfield University
Saturday, October 26, 11:00 a.m. - 12 noon

AFTER SCHOOL COURSES

These lecture classes are offered in conjunction with the School of the Pennsylvania Academy of the Fine Arts and open to the general public. Many school districts accept these courses for in-service credit. Please check with your local district. For registration please send your check payable to *The Pennsylvania Academy of the Fine Arts*, to the Saturday and Evening Programs Office, or call 972-7632 for Visa/Mastercard payment.

FALL 1991

Every Picture Tells a Story, Four Mondays; the history of narrative art.
September 16, 23, 30 and October 7,
5:30 - 7:00 p.m. $48 registration fee.

Furniture in the Making, Four Wednesdays; an overview of American studio furniture development in the twentieth-century. October 2, 9, 16, and 23.
5:30 - 7:00 p.m., $48 registration fee.

Eakins and American Realism, Four Tuesdays; examines the American Master in the context of a major art movement.
November 5, 12, 19, and 26, 5:30 - 7:00 p.m.
$48 registration fee.

SPRING 1992

Thomas Eakins: Philadelphia Painter,
Four Tuesdays; four scholars present different aspects of the artist's life and work.
February 4, 11, 18, and 25, 5:30 - 7:00 p.m.
$48 registration fee.

Birds of a Feather, Four Thursdays; focuses on four American artists: Eakins, Homer, Chase, and Sargent.
March 5, 12, 19, and 26, 5:30 - 7:00 p.m.
$48 registration fee.

ART AFTER SCHOOL

Poets, Palaces, and Porcupines. A seven week program for children 8 - 12 years old. Designed to enhance the art and museum experience, this class will combine gallery exploration and studio art projects.
October 3, 10, 17, 24, 31, November 7, 14. $40 per student (general public), $35 (museum members). Please make check payable to *The Pennsylvania Academy of the Fine Arts*. For more information call: 972-7608.

FAMILY PROGRAMS

are offered on Saturdays at 11:00 a.m. throughout the year. There is a $2 materials fee per participant. Call 972-7608 for further information.

For a current brochure of our many studio and lecture courses, call the office of Saturday and Evening Programs at 972-7632.

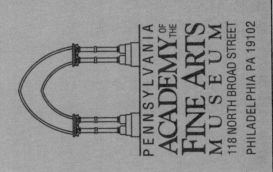

PENNSYLVANIA
ACADEMY OF THE
FINE ARTS
M U S E U M
118 NORTH BROAD STREET
PHILADELPHIA PA 19102

creative SCIENCE TEACHING

FREE WORKSHOPS FOR TEACHERS

Through the generosity of the Philadelphia Electric Company and The Dairy Council, Inc.. The Academy of Natural Sciences is again providing its successful Teacher Workshop series FREE OF CHARGE during the 1990-91 school year.

Tales, Tunes, and Trade Books

Date: Saturday, January 12, 1991
Time: 10:00 AM to 4:00 PM
Audience: Elementary and middle school teachers

DESCRIPTION: Learn how to integrate environmental education into your classroom curriculum through the use of children's literature, storytelling, slide presentations, craft activities, and song. Each technique will be demonstrated and participants will be actively involved throughout the workshop. Dozens of children's books will be available for discussion and review; several handouts and bibliographies will be distributed as well. Come dressed to play!
Instructor: Scott Palermo, *School Psychologist, The Port Jarvis School District*

Sharing Science With Young Children

Date: Saturday, January 26, 1991
Time: 10:00 AM to 12:00 PM
Audience: Lower elementary school teachers

DESCRIPTION: Titles such as "Grab a Shape," "The Toilet Paper Roll Looker," "Paint a Color Brighter," and "The Shiny Solution" characterize many of the activities introduced and experienced in this workshop. The instructor will offer three levels of expertise: an overview of basic scientific processes (observation, classification, measuring, etc.), suggestions on how to introduce these concepts to very young children, and specific hands-on endeavors designed to engage and enlighten.
Instructor: Jonah Roll, *Curator of Education, The Museum of the Philadelphia Civic Center*

REGISTRATION INFORMATION

1. Please refer to "audience" to determine which workshops are recommended (but not restricted to) which grade levels.

2. Interested teachers must register by mail. Completed registration forms should be sent to "Creative Science Teaching," Academy of Natural Sciences, 19th & The Parkway, Philadelphia, PA 19103.

3. A refundable registration fee of $10 per workshop, paid by check or credit card, must accompany the registration form. This has become necessary in order to ensure maximum workshop attendance.

4. Registration fees will be returned, in May, at the conclusion of the 1990/91 workshop series.

5. Participants are strongly encouraged to attend each session of a multi-session workshop.

6. Cancellations must be made at least one week in advance of a single or multi-session workshop. Persons cancelling within one week of a workshop will not be eligible for a refund.

7. Individuals will be registered on a first-come, first-served basis.

8. Confirmation or waiting-list letters will be mailed upon receipt of registration. Confirmation letters will include additional information and details (meeting place, recommended dress, parking suggestions, etc.)

9. In-service credit is available for teachers taking 15 or more hours of Creative Science Teaching. Please call Nancy Darmstadter, at 299-1061, for information.

10. For additional questions or information, please call 299-1054.

CREATIVE SCIENCE TEACHING REGISTRATION FORM

Date _____

Name _____

Address _____ City _____

State _____ Zip _____

Phone (Day) _____ (Evening) ____

School Address _____

Grade(s) taught _____

Subject(s) _____

Workshop Title(s)

___ From Moo to You: Cows, Food, and Nutrition
___ Dinosaurs in Your Classroom
___ Rock-Bottom Earth Science
___ The Sun as the Source
___ Tales, Tunes, and Trade Books
___ Sharing Science with Young Children
___ Live Animals in the Classroom
___ Hot Topics in Environmental Science
___ Healthy Dividends
___ Crystals to Continents
___ The Do-It-Yourself Science Exposition
___ Energy and the Way We Live
___ Weather Wise and Wherefores

Enclosed is $ _____ to cover the cost of _____ workshop registrations.

☐ I have included a check payable to The Academy of Natural Sciences.

Please charge my ☐ MasterCard ☐ Visa

Credit Card Number _____

Expiration Date _____

Signature _____

Please mail to:
CREATIVE SCIENCE TEACHING
The Academy of Natural Sciences
19th and The Parkway
Philadelphia, PA 19103

Visual Arts as Sources for Teaching

VAST

Philadelphia Museum of Art

JUST FOR TEACHERS

ACCREDITED INSERVICE COURSE

The museum's Division of Education offers single-credit inservice courses for teachers through the Allegheny Intermediate Unit. This fall the one-credit course "All About Rocks and Minerals" will be held at the museum on three Saturdays: October 6, 20, and 27. This course will utilize the resources of the museum to help elementary and middle school teachers develop science units about rocks and minerals. Registration is being handled by the Allegheny Intermediate Unit. For further information call the AIU's Continuing Professional Education Department at (412) 394-5762.

CUSTOMIZED INSERVICE PROGRAMS

Why not plan your school's inservice at the museum? A 3½-hour inservice program introducing the museum's educational resources and how to use them can be tailored to your needs. The agenda includes a tour of selected exhibits, details of the museum-based and outreach programs available to teachers, and lesson ideas. The fee for this 3½-hour program for a maximum of 25 teachers is $90. Call 622-3375 or 622-3292 to discuss your needs and reserve a date.

See page 6 for information about the **Ninth Annual Educational Loan Collection Open House and Workshop**.

Teacher Workshops 1992–93

Philadelphia Museum of Art

Teacher

Four Centuries of Art: A Global View

Saturdays: 10:00 a.m.–3:00 p.m.

Part One
The 16th and 17th Centuries

October 10	Venice and Tenochtitlán
October 24	Beijing and Benin
November 14	Madrid and Isfahan
November 21	Amsterdam and Native American Nations

Part Two
The 18th and 19th Centuries

January 16	Philadelphia and St. Petersburg
January 30	Athens and Edo, Japan
February 13	Paris and Bombay
February 27	Rio de Janeiro and New York

What were the artistic trends in 16th-century Tenochtitlán (Mexico City) while Titian was painting in Venice, or in Isfahan while Rembrandt worked in 17th-century Amsterdam? What were artists doing in St. Petersburg while Charles Willson Peale worked in 18th-century Philadelphia or in Bombay while Pissarro painted in 19th-century Paris? This two-part course will examine in each century four widely divergent contemporary civilizations and the achievements of their artists.

Each workshop will begin with an informal coffee and discussion period, followed by two-and-one-half hours of public slide lectures on the topics listed above. After lunch, teachers and Museum staff members will spend a final hour in the galleries discussing techniques for engaging students in the art of these time periods.

Cost:
Part One: Members $100 non-members $150
Part Two: Members $100 non-members $150
Parts One and Two: Members $175 non-members $275

Credit: One Pennsylvania in-service credit may be obtained for each part of this course.

Teacher Workshop Registration Form

Name

Complete address

Home phone

School phone

School

Subject

Grade

School district

I.U.

I would like to receive in-service credit

Social Security #

Please circle courses you want:

Four Centuries of Art: A Global View
Part I $
Part II $
Parts I & II $

**Leonardo da Vinci: The Anatomy of Man;
Drawings from the Collection of Her
Majesty Queen Elizabeth II** $

Martin Puryear $

**The Impressionist and the City:
Pissarro's Series** $

**Workers: The End of Manual Labor:
Photographs of Sebastião Salgado** $

Total $

Non-refundable tuition is payable by check to the Philadelphia Museum of Art.

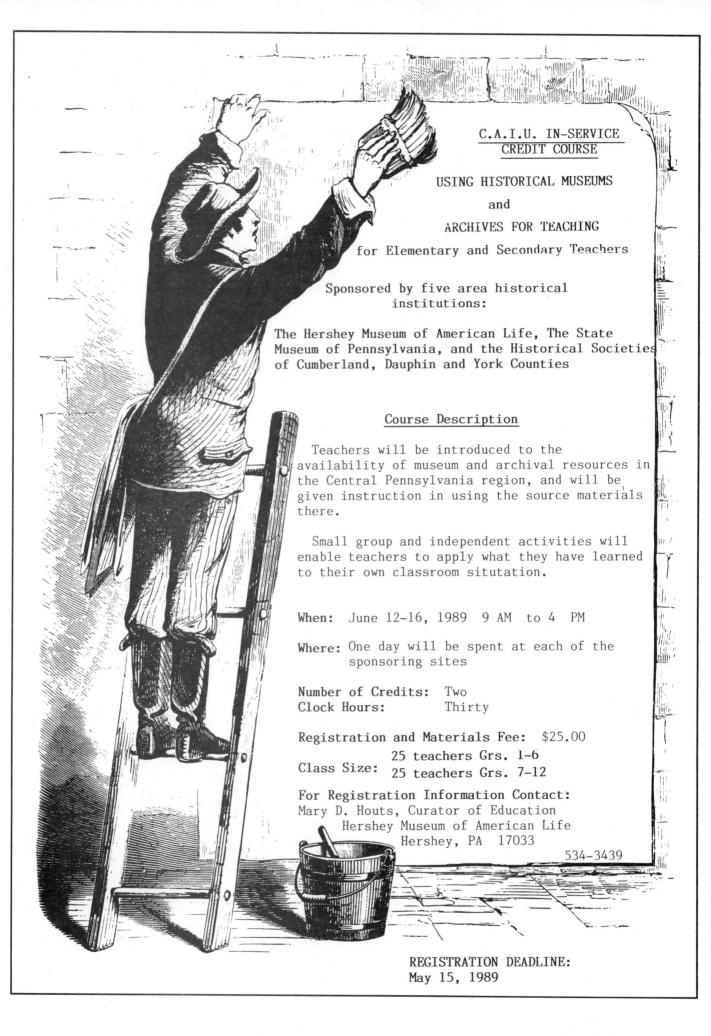

C.A.I.U. IN-SERVICE
CREDIT COURSE

USING HISTORICAL MUSEUMS

and

ARCHIVES FOR TEACHING

for Elementary and Secondary Teachers

Sponsored by five area historical institutions:

The Hershey Museum of American Life, The State Museum of Pennsylvania, and the Historical Societies of Cumberland, Dauphin and York Counties

Course Description

Teachers will be introduced to the availability of museum and archival resources in the Central Pennsylvania region, and will be given instruction in using the source materials there.

Small group and independent activities will enable teachers to apply what they have learned to their own classroom situtation.

When: June 12-16, 1989 9 AM to 4 PM

Where: One day will be spent at each of the sponsoring sites

Number of Credits: Two
Clock Hours: Thirty

Registration and Materials Fee: $25.00

Class Size: 25 teachers Grs. 1-6
25 teachers Grs. 7-12

For Registration Information Contact:
Mary D. Houts, Curator of Education
    Hershey Museum of American Life
        Hershey, PA 17033

534-3439

REGISTRATION DEADLINE:
May 15, 1989

AAM Membership Information

Individual AAM Membership

MUSEUM STAFF AND MUSEUM ASSOCIATION STAFF

(PAID OR UNPAID)

DUES ARE BASED ON ANNUAL INCOME.

PLEASE CHECK ONE:

- ❑ $55,001 OR MORE $125
- ❑ $45,001-55,000 $105
- ❑ $35,001-45,000 $85
- ❑ $25,001-35,000 $65
- ❑ $20,001-25,000 $55
- ❑ $15,001-20,000 $45
- ❑ $15,000 OR LESS $35
- ❑ NON-PAID STAFF $25
- ❑ TRUSTEE $100

AFFILIATED INDIVIDUAL CATEGORIES

- ❑ STUDENT* [PLEASE SEND COPY OF VALID I.D.] $25
- ❑ RETIRED MUSEUM STAFF / TRUSTEE* $25
  - *CHOOSE ONE: ❑ MUSEUM NEWS ❑ AVISO
- ❑ LIBRARIAN / ACADEMICIAN $35
- ❑ PRESS / PUBLIC $35
- ❑ INDEPENDENT PROFESSIONAL:
  - ❑ INCOME $25,000 OR OVER $125
  - ❑ INCOME UNDER $25,000 $65

(FOR-PROFIT INDIVIDUALS SUPPLYING GOODS AND/OR SERVICES TO THE MUSEUM FIELD ARE INELIGIBLE FOR MUSEUM STAFF MEMBERSHIP AND MUST JOIN AS **INDEPENDENT PROFESSIONALS.** THIS CATEGORY INCLUDES SELF-EMPLOYED INDIVIDUALS.)

NAME

TITLE

INSITUTIONAL AFFILIATION**

MAILING ADDRESS

CITY, STATE, ZIP

TELEPHONE

FAX

**PLEASE INDICATE AFFILIATION OR EXPLANATION OF CURRENT STATUS. FAILURE TO DO SO WILL DELAY PROCESSING OF YOUR APPLICATION.

MEMBERSHIP IN AAM INCLUDES $19 FROM ANNUAL MEMBERSHIP DUES APPLICABLE TO A SUBSCRIPTION TO MUSEUM NEWS, EXCEPT FOR STUDENTS AND RETIREES. DUES SUBJECT TO CHANGE WITHOUT NOTICE.

Institutional AAM Membership

MUSEUMS AND RELATED ORGANIZATIONS

DUES ARE BASED ON ANNUAL OPERATING BUDGET.
MINIMUM DUES ARE $75. MAXIMUM DUES ARE $15,000.
MUSEUM BUDGET $ _____ MULTIPLIED BY .001 = $_____
❑ NONPROFIT   ❑ FOR-PROFIT

I AM AUTHORIZED TO REQUEST AAM MEMBERSHIP FOR THIS INSTITUTION.

SIGNATURE

AFFILIATED COMMERCIAL ORGANIZATIONS

- ❑ FIRM [BENEFITS FOR 2 PEOPLE] $350
- ❑ ADDITIONAL STAFF $100

ORGANIZATION

CONTACT PERSON

MAILING ADDRESS

CITY, STATE, ZIP

DAY TELEPHONE

SECOND PERSON—FIRM ONLY

MAILING ADDRESS

CITY, STATE, ZIP

TELEPHONE

FAX

PAYMENT:

AMOUNT $_____
❑ CHECK MADE PAYABLE TO AAM   ❑ VISA   ❑ MASTERCARD

CARD NUMBER

CARD EXPIRATION DATE

SIGNATURE

PLEASE SEND FORM AND PAYMENT TO:
AMERICAN ASSOCIATION OF MUSEUMS
DEPT. 4002, WASHINGTON, DC 20042-4002